COOPERATIVE COMMUNITIES

HOW TO START THEM, AND WHY

COOPERATIVE COMMUNITIES — HOW TO START THEM, AND WHY

by

Swami Kriyananda

ANANDA PUBLICATIONS
Alleghany Star Route
Nevada City, California 95959

Second edition, 1968
Third edition, 1969
Fourth edition, 1970
Fifth edition, 1970
Sixth edition, 1971

Printed in the United States of America

This book is lovingly dedicated to my spiritual teacher, Paramahansa Yogananda, who envisioned cooperative communities as one of the solutions to the problems nowadays besetting mankind.

Other books by Swami Kriyananda include:

Yours—the Universe!
Yoga Postures for Self-Awareness
Your Sun Sign as a Spiritual Guide
and other works.

For information, write to the publishers.

PREFACE TO THE SIXTH EDITION

"Everyone talks about the weather, but nobody ever *does* anything about it!" This familiar joke might be paraphrased and applied to countless books that have been written about utopian communities. Most of them are indeed utopias (a Greek word meaning, *nowhere*). They have been food for dreams, but almost never for action.

In that sense, this little book is an exception. It was written primarily for people who want to do something about the ideas it presents. It was written also as a handbook for a community that I myself was planning to start. And it is an exception, finally, because that project, called Ananda Cooperative Community, actually did get started, and after three years is still thriving.

In earlier editions of this book it was premature for me to say much about Ananda as a living laboratory for the ideas here presented. The ideas themselves were the fruit of many years of thought, study, and experience; I felt reasonably confident in sharing them with the reader. Ananda, however, was still too fledgling a community for its experiences to add anything substantial to this book.

Since then, however, the situation has changed. Ananda has struggled; it has erred; it has grown. Its experiences have caused me to rewrite certain portions of this book with a view to making it more practical.

In addition to theory, moreover, I have enlarged this sixth edition to include a whole second section on the history of Ananda, and on the special lessons we have learned here. Ours is, to be sure, only one example of a central idea that may be developed in many different directions. Nevertheless, our actual experiences may help to clarify some of the suggestions made in the first part of this book. In this sense our experiences, though perhaps uniquely our own, may also serve a more universal purpose.

TABLE OF CONTENTS

INTRODUCTION

To the best of my recollection, I first became interested in cooperative communities when I was fifteen years old. The year was 1941. World War II was raging in Europe. The world that I had known there as a child was disintegrating in ruins and mass hatreds. To me it seemed that the passions that had been unleashed would never spend themselves in a single war.

At this time I wrote a one-act play called *The Peace Treaty*. It concerned a meeting of a group of cave men, the leaders of several allied tribes that had just won a war, to discuss how future peace might be ensured. The meeting began hopefully, with idealistic talk of brotherhood and forgiveness. Gradually, however, the desire for self-aggrandizement, presented self-righteously as a wish to "discipline" the enemy, forced the writing of a completely oppressive document, no "peace treaty" at all, but certain to sow seeds of future conflict. Offstage at the end of the play one heard shouts, and the striking of club on club; then, progressively, the twanging of bowstrings, the popping of muskets, cannon fire, the chatter of machine guns, the bursting of bombs – and, finally, one huge explosion. And then – silence.

It was in this apocalyptic mood, when I was still fifteen, that I set out to write a utopian novel about a group of people who, convinced that civilization was about to bomb itself back to the caves, set off for a remote spot in South America to escape the devastation. They consisted of people skilled in various civilized disciplines: science, engineering, the arts. Their goal was to keep the lamp of civilization burning brightly through the Dark Age to come. They would also, I'm sure, have evolved The Perfect Society – if only I had completed the book! Unfortunately, my imagination proved unequal to the task. Or perhaps I was already beginning to sense the absurdity of trying to perfect anything so inherently unstable as human society.

At any rate, I was certainly not disillusioned with the whole communal idea. I even tried to persuade some of my friends to help me to carry it out. (Imagine, if you can, a group of fifteen-year-old "specialists" in various branches of science, engineering, and the arts!) Their enthusiasm was high until they realized that I was quite in earnest. Their subsequent apathy only prodded me toward greater maturity in my thinking.

But I have never held with people who equate maturity with cynicism. Shortly after I graduated from high school, I attended a two-week peace conference. One day there, a woman guest speaker gave us an enthusiastic report on cooperative societies. The subject was too fascinating for me to be left, as it seemed, "in the air." During the question-and-answer period that followed, I stood up and, not at all cynically, requested a more rounded picture. "You've explained the advantages of these cooperatives," I said. "I wonder if you would speak to us also of some of their *dis*advantages?"

The woman was flabbergasted at my impertinence. "Why," she spluttered, "there are *no* disadvantages!"

Whereupon she lost what may have been her most interested listener. For the thought of *anything* in this mixed-bag of a world having no disadvantages at all was, to me by this time, preposterous. My future study of the subject, and finally the writing of this book, was guided always by a search merely for *better* alternatives, not for perfect ones.

In college I came to believe more and more strongly in personal transformation as the key to any real social change. Social uplift, I now saw, must come from the inner consciousness of individuals; it cannot be inspired by outward legislation, nor by any mass approach to human problems. A widespread transformation of consciousness was, I felt, more likely to be initiated in small communities of idealistic men and women than in large, heterogeneous urban communities.

Thus it was that my early vision of escapist colonies evolved into one in which small communities played a vital and responsible role in the present-day world. But still I looked to an outward system as the primary means of changing the inner man. Still, therefore, my vision was naive.

While I searched more and more for the means to human betterment, everyone else my own age seemed to be thinking increasingly of such practical matters as getting a job, raising a family, becoming rich and important. Whenever I spoke to any of them of my community ideas, their usual response was to look at one another strangely and say, "What's the matter with *him*?"

And so it was that my search for a better social

system became channeled toward a search for personal upliftment. The essential thing for me, I now realized, as the one individual over whom I had any measurable influence, was to change myself. This soon came to mean for me nothing less than a search for inner enlightenment.

I was fortunate at this time in my life (it was in September, 1948) to meet that great master of yoga, Paramahansa Yogananda (the author of *Autobiography of a Yogi*), and to be accepted by him as a disciple. For years thereafter I devoted myself, under his guidance, to yoga practices of meditation. After the first year or so he gave me the duty also of teaching those practices around the world.

A search for inner enlightenment need not conflict with a concern for social upliftment. Rather, it is the only valid key to upliftment of any kind. I was thrilled to discover that my Guru, too, dreamed of founding communities similar to those I had envisioned, based on mutual cooperation and on harmonious, spiritual living. He actually listed this as one of fourteen basic points in his life mission.

But he was unable, in the short span of an incredibly productive life, to put his communal scheme into practice. It was not, indeed, the central point of his mission, and to the best of my knowledge his other disciples generally have not shown very much interest in it. It was a keen interest of mine, however, long before I met him. His words only fanned an existing flame.

Thus, presumptuously perhaps, I came to feel personally responsible for the fulfillment of this aspect of his work. I studied whatever literature I could find on the subject. For years I mulled over the pros and cons of communal living. I sounded out economists, businessmen, teachers, political thinkers. I visited a kibbutz in Israel, and two well-known communities in India: Dayalbagh, near Agra, and the Sri Aurobindo ashram in Pondicherry. Most instructive of all were fourteen years that I spent in my Guru's monasteries in America and in India. Monastic life offers valuable lessons in the difficulties and advantages of any communal form of living. At an early stage of my life there I was placed in charge of the other monks, and came thereby to learn at first hand many of the problems to be faced in coordinating such a community.

In spite of all this thinking, study, and experience, in spite even of my most recent undertaking in actually founding a community myself, I dare not promise the reader more than an interesting introduction to a vitally promising idea. Cooperative communities cannot be perfected on paper, nor even in any one community. They are made up of people, and must be expected to vary in ways too numerous to mention, even as people do. My hope in this book, then, is to set into motion the wheels of individual interest – as a first step, perhaps, to what may become individual involvement.

Swami Kriyananda

Ananda Cooperative Community
Nevada City, California, U.S.A.

PART I

Chapter One

THE TIME IS NOW

In his last years on earth, the great teacher, Paramahansa Yogananda, repeatedly and urgently spoke of a plan that he said was destined to become a basic social pattern for the new age: the formation of Self-realization cooperative communities, or "World Brotherhood Colonies." In almost every public lecture, no matter what his announced subject, he would digress to urge people to act upon his proposal.

"The day will come," he predicted, "when this idea will spread through the world like wildfire. Gather together, those of you who share high ideals. Pool your resources. Buy land in the country. A simple life will bring you inner freedom. Harmony with nature will bring you a happiness known to few city dwellers. In the company of other truth seekers it will be easier for you to meditate and to think of God.

"What is the need for all the luxury with which people surround themselves? Most of what they have they are paying for on the installment plan. Their debts are a source of unending worry to them. Even people whose luxuries have been paid for are not free. Attachment makes them slaves. They consider themselves freer for their possessions, and don't see how their possessions in turn have possessed them!"

Yogananda stressed the joys of simple, natural living and God thinking – a way of life that, he said, would bring people "happiness and freedom." But his message went beyond simply presenting people with an attractive idea. There was an urgency in his plea.

"The time is short," he repeatedly told his audiences. "You have no idea of the sufferings that await mankind. In addition to wars there will be a depression the like of which has not been known in a very long time. Money will not be worth the paper it is printed on. Millions will die."

Again he said: "You don't know what a terrible cataclysm is coming!"

To place reliance upon prophetic utterances may strike some people as superstitious. Even these people, however, may be interested to note that, of persons reputed to have prophetic vision, every single one has predicted terrible sufferings for humanity in the years to come.* But it is not necessary to rely blindly on their prophecies. The events they have predicted are already too visibly probable.

Numerous biologists have stated with absolute finality that the present population explosion can have only one result: In the few years to come (quite possibly, they say, as early as 1975) "hundreds of millions" of people in the world must either die of starvation for lack of sufficient food on our planet to feed them, or be destroyed in a nuclear holocaust as they struggle for whatever food they can get. Economic depression of massive proportions has been predicted by reputable

*Bhrigu, an Indian sage, wrote: "There will be weeping in every home."

economists. And as for warfare, one must, of course, always hope for the best – but what real chances are there, think you, for a cessation of conflict? The pressures continue to mount. They have not lessened, even with the threat of global destruction.

Let us consider the solution that Yogananda proposed – that of Self-realization cooperatives, or "world brotherhood colonies." It was, to be sure, a personal, not a universal solution that he was stressing. Yet many universal changes have proceeded from personal transformations. (Witness the widespread upliftment that grew out of the teachings of Buddha and Jesus Christ. The ensuing social revolutions were out of all proportion to the few disciples converted by those great masters.)

There is, moreover, at this time in history, an implication in this idea of communal cooperatives that lifts it quite out of the personal category into something sociological and universal.

Chapter Two

SELF-REALIZATION VS. THE MEGALOPOLIS

No one needs a sociologist to tell him that the trend of this twentieth century is toward consolidation. Small businesses, unable to compete with the large corporations, become swallowed up by them. Large corporations, again, merge with others, in time to become vast industrial empires.

Societies of men are moving inexorably toward a centralization of power. The world's increasing population necessitates increasing government control. The old argument between states' rights and federal rights is an anachronism. It is impossible, legislatively and economically, nowadays to return the power to local governments. The trend, instead, is toward a consolidation not only of cities and states, but of countries.

What will the result of all this consolidation be for man, the individual?

It is in the interest of economy and efficiency that separate groups of people unite. The danger is that those same principles, economy and efficiency, will demand of people a uniformity that extends to their personal lives. Numerous social thinkers have noted that individual tastes and values, too, must be, and *are* being, increasingly subordinated to the institutional order – the "Establishment."

To the institutional mind, such uniformity may seem an end and a blessing in itself. Selfish individualism is decried by such people, and of course rightly so. But consolidation is posed by them as the only alternative, and anyone supporting such a trend is hailed as a "liberal."

Is it truly liberal to destroy human liberty? Voluntary cooperation is one thing; enforced uniformity, quite another.

There is a third alternative open to man. *It lies in a recognition of the fact that the mainspring of mature action is the inner man, not an outer order.*

To imagine that systems can be anything more than a convenience has been man's mistake. Systems are not an end in themselves. They cannot inspire men to perfection. At best, they may prevent a few people from behaving too outrageously.

The more society becomes centralized in its power, the greater the need for individuals to seek their values (as opposed to their outer convenience) *within themselves.* For man is more than a cog in the social wheel. The systems he adopts are supposed in some way to benefit *him*, individually, and not some separate entity, unrelated to any of its members, called, "Society." To speak of society, as some writers have done, as an "organism," is misleading. From *within* ourselves come our inspiration, our understanding, our love and happiness. All that we experience outside depends upon our inner *capacity* for experience. Man is a *source* of light, not a mirror.

Thus, the point must come in modern social evolution when men, instead of succumbing placidly to the outward demand for uniformity, rise up individually to reassert their dignity as human beings.

The trend of which we speak is inevitable. In fact, it has already begun. We see it in the revolution of the young – in the beatniks, the hippies, the "forest people," as also in the wide-spread and growing interest in meditation, in Zen Buddhism, in yoga. In communistic countries the governments have tried to curb this tendency, but even there it is clearly in evidence.

It was even in evidence in the utterly dehumanizing atmosphere of the World War II concentration camps. Even there, individuals could be found who, in personal resistance to the sordid influences around them, rose like lotuses from the mud and blossomed into greatness.

It is time to press forward from a preoccupation with outward systems to a recognition of the real key to the efficacy of any system: individual man. The need of the hour is for self-unfoldment – not as a selfish imposition on the universe (the "Great God, EGO" of Ayn Rand) – but simply as a private and deeply personal search for Self-realization.

The result cannot but benefit man in his political, economic, and social institutions as well. For all things bring harmony to men who have found inner harmony. And nothing brings it to men in whom inner discord prevails.

The question arises: How, without imposing on anyone else, may one develop an inner life in the midst of social confusion? It is difficult to have inner peace when one is surrounded by chaos. It is difficult to progress steadily in one direction through swirling currents that lead off in a million other directions.

Consider: What need is there to cling to city life? If it doesn't happen to suit one, what moral end can be served by sticking grimly to it? The chance that somehow it may be molded in time to become a universal blessing? It is not his systems that bless man, but man who blesses his systems by having the good will to make them work.

No, it is not necessary from any standpoint – social, philosophical, personal – to remain in an environ-

Farming at Ananda. The arched structure is where Ananda incense is made.

ment that is not conducive to one's own welfare. For the man of aspiring mind, the megalopolis of modern times ceases to be what it is for so many people: a convenience. It becomes, instead, an obstruction. He must find his way, just as soon as circumstances allow him to do so, to the sanity and peace of a simpler way of life.

A person who devotes himself to the development of an inner awareness is in a vastly better position than one who, his very self-respect assaulted by competing hordes, has all he can do to maintain a little sense of his own identity.

One reads with horror various newspaper accounts of people who watched calmly, refusing to become involved, as some major crime was committed, or as someone fell and died in the street. It would seem that the average city dweller's technique for preserving his own sanity is to isolate himself from the vast universe around him, and from his fellow man. Stranded and alone on the tiny island of his ego, is it any wonder that alienation has become such a common complaint?

"This above all," Shakespeare wrote, "to thine own self be true, and it must follow, as the night the day, thou canst not then be false to any man." Without self-respect, how can there be a proper respect for other men? Without self-awareness, how can there be a sensitivity to the needs of others? The well-springs of charity must flow from the inner man. They cannot reach him by a process of invasion.

To "hie away" to the country, then, need in no way imply a rejection of one's social responsibilities. It can become, rather, the beginning of a sincere assumption of such responsibilities.

Chapter Three

COOPERATIVE COMMUNITIES AND THE QUEST FOR OPPORTUNITY

Why do people move to the city? The main reasons are not difficult to find. Here, jobs are more plentiful, social life is more varied, cultural stimuli are incomparably greater than in rural areas.

Country living, by contrast, whatever its natural appeal, poses severe obstacles for the average person. Economic opportunities, as far as he is concerned, are minimal. He is not a farmer even by inclination. The skills he has developed are city skills: The merchant who needs customers for his wares, the secretary who needs letters to type, and the teacher who needs students to teach. Any move on his own to the country would require total re-education, and perhaps, for all that, a life of relative uselessness.

And what of social opportunities? If he has no taste for farming, he is not likely to want to spend his leisure time hobnobbing with people whose chief discussion centers on the state of the season's crops.

What comes hardly on one's own, however, is not difficult to accomplish in a group. Persons of like interest, banding together in communities, preserving their customary inter-dependence, each contributing to the whole, perhaps with modifications, his accustomed skills – under such circumstances, there is no reason why the city person need feel out of place.

Consider, in this context, the simple question of artistic and intellectual opportunities.

In variety, no small community could compete with the big city. But the greatest satisfaction in the arts lies in creating, not merely in being entertained. In this area the intentional community could offer incomparably more: the time to create, a sympathetic audience, inspiring natural surroundings, an opportunity to explore and develop one's inner life.

Nor need a variety of stimulation be lacking. A community accustomed to good libraries would find sufficient incentive to create one of its own. Outside lecturers could be invited to come and speak. An occasional outing to the city to attend a symphony concert or an art exhibit would afford as much cultural exposure as most city dwellers get.

There is no reason why a community seeking a natural way of life should utterly reject modern civilization. Perfect isolation would be economically unsound even if it were in some way desirable. Unless one wanted to revert to a bleakly primitive existence, complete self-sufficiency would mean that a community would have to produce, at enormous expense, all of its own machinery, its plumbing fixtures, its cooking and eating utensils, its clothing fabrics, even its own toothpaste. Considering how inexpensive such items become when produced on a mass scale, it seems only practical for a community to devote itself to selling what it can on the outside, and to buying what it needs with the profit.

The community might, in short, be similar in many

ways to any village, with the basic distinction that it would be an *intentional* community, based on cooperation, not competition, on self-unfoldment rather than on self-aggrandizement at the expense of one's fellows.

Basic to the success of any community is the question of income. People living together cooperatively in the country could grow their own food, build their own buildings, perhaps make their own clothes, but many of the materials even for these basic necessities would have to be brought in from outside. What possible sources of income would there be for a community living well outside the busy industrial centers? The problem is not so difficult as it may seem.

Presumably, persons coming to live in the community would bring with them certain skills, for some of which – wood carving, painting, weaving, sandle-making, pottery – a ready market could be found in the nearby cities.

Specialization is the hallmark of our age. It should not be difficult for creative minds to find some sort of industry in which the community could specialize, offering its product at a competitive price to the industrial, building, or mercantile world – the manufacture, for example, of electronic devices.

Books could be published, clothing made, records produced, a mail order business developed, all of which could bring income to the community.

A major source of income could be weekend programs and seminars for outsiders.

Another possible source of income, and something that would in any case be necessary, would be a school for children. A school run on creative and idealistic lines should attract students from outside the community.

The community could also create its own dramas, pageants, and other artistic and spiritual entertainments, which it would be in a position to offer to clubs, schools, and colleges around the country.

There is no reason why the community could not also open its own stores in surrounding cities. Integrity of workmanship, and lower costs resulting from the elimination of middlemen, should make it possible to win for its products a good enough reputation to ensure their commercial success.

Basic to the economic success of a cooperative community would be the simple principle of cooperation. In the big cities, every man is obliged to compete for his place in the sun. Out of a thousand people, each has 999 rivals. Anxiety, tension, frustration – these are a few of the known side effects. But consider also how much time and energy are devoted in ordinary business to outmaneuvering, outbidding, and out-shouting the other fellow, and how much money is spent for the ungenerous purpose of drawing shoppers away from his door to one's own.

Much has been written about the benefits of a competitive system. Certainly, the huge socialistic monopoly that is normally posed as an alternative, while it may result in less material waste, affords also less human incentive. But what of the small intentional community, where *voluntary cooperation* is taught as an alternative to both competition and monopoly?

Supposing that out of a thousand people, each person had, not 999 rivals, but as many friends and co-workers? There is no reason why this should not be possible in a community that emphasized cooperation as a way of life. I myself lived in such a community for ten years. It was the headquarters of Self-Realization

Fellowship in Los Angeles, the organization founded by my spiritual teacher, Paramahansa Yogananda. Among eighty or more people living and working at close quarters there was scarcely ever any friction, and a tremendous amount of work was accomplished. Assuredly, cooperation is more than a dream.

The fact is that cooperative communities of the past have already demonstrated considerable financial stability. Where they have failed, the fault has been largely an impractical effort to isolate themselves, or too idealistic an expectation of human nature.

But cooperation, ideally understood, should by no means be limited to the community. It should reach out to embrace the larger "community" of mankind. Hence, of course, the term, "world brotherhood colony."

In India, the devout Hindu is taught, before he eats his meal, to pour a libation of gratitude onto the ground from which his food has come, to give food to the animals with whose help he obtained it, and to feed the hungry stranger whose position, but for good fortune, he might himself be sharing. Side by side, similarly, with a search for personal and communal prosperity, there should develop a sense of responsibility to the world at large, without whose existence the community would be little more than a barbaric tribe.

Instead of competition with the outside world, there should develop a sense of sharing with it. One important contribution might be that of example.

Two donkeys were harnessed by a peasant to move a rock. But the animals pulled in opposite directions. While they worked themselves to exhaustion, the rock was not moved an inch. What of a community where men have learned to act in a spirit of cooperation, not of ceaseless competition – where a little labor suffices to feed many mouths? Would such an example be totally lost on society at large?

Rome and Carthage, fighting one another to their mutual destruction, set an example for the ages of the uselessness of selfish greed. But better than ten negative examples is one positive solution. What of a community that views others, not as competitors or as strangers, but as friends? Such a community, even though removed from the vortices of civilization, could be a more forceful influence for good than a dozen institutions that are more "involved," but also more submerged, in the urban insanities.

Chapter Four

COOPERATIVE COMMUNITIES, PAST AND PRESENT

A remark that one often hears with respect to cooperative communities is, "So many have been started, but all of them have failed." This statement is not true. Actually, there have been a number of spectacular successes.

The Inspirationists of Amana, the Harmonists at Economy, the Menonites, the Shakers, the Hutterites – these names are well known to history. They were wealthy. Some of them are still flourishing. That others eventually died out – often after decades, even after one or two centuries – need no more be termed a failure than the eventual death of countless business concerns. The way of life is ever to grow, then die. Without eventual death, room would never be made for new life forms. If an institution endures through the ages, in fact, it is probably because at some point in its history it chose, instead of dying, to become petrified.

In our own age we have only to look at the Kibbutzim of modern Israel to see a vital, flourishing movement that, for all its ups and downs, cannot in any way be termed a failure.

And there are the monasteries, similar in some ways, if not in all, to cooperative communities.

It would be wise briefly to consider various communal experiments, to learn why some of them failed, and why others were successful.

Often, as we have already said, the unsuccessful experiments were founded on too idealistic a view of human nature. A reading of *Kibbutz*, by Melford E. Spiro, conveys the impression that even the modern Kibbutzim, while in themselves a decided success, have proved disillusioning to some of their members, who expected their way of life to evolve the "perfect" man. Rousseau's concept of "the noble savage" reads well in print, but one encounters this wonderful creature all too rarely here on ignoble earth. The jungle savage is often *less* noble than his city counterpart. The belief that a return to nature will automatically produce saints is naive. The ensuing disappointment can well prove shattering.

Linked to too idealistic a view of human nature was the failure of communities – devastating to any but the best established – to screen their applicants. Robert Owen, in founding a utopian community at New Harmony, Pennsylvania, did not take into account the danger of mixing people of diverse convictions. His community lasted only three years.

Perhaps one of the greatest mistakes that community planners made was to hope too much from their plans. No system can create virtue. The most it can do is facilitate the development of virtue, for virtue is a development that must always spring from the good will of the individual members. "Freeland," a community founded in the 1890's on the basis of a book by the Austrian economist, Theodor Hertzka, failed largely for this reason. In trying to adhere too closely to Hertzka's elaborate blueprint, the community finally foundered in disillusionment.

A common failing of new communities has been the tendency to demand too radical a change of their members. In biology there is an axiom that nature never proceeds by sudden leaps. This is certainly true, with very rare exceptions, of human nature. Leniency must be granted people, within reason, to grow at their own rate of speed.

Another defect in certain communal experiments has been a tendency to isolationism. A group of people that seek to cut off all ties with the outside world will find themselves forced to work tirelessly simply to produce the bare necessities. One generation may be inspired, in reaction against modern life, to withdraw to such extremes. But unless their children are kept exceedingly uninformed, the chances are that when they grow up they will want to return to the cities, where at least one does not have to slave like a beast of burden merely to maintain his existence.

The consensus of persons who have made a study of community life is that some definite communal structure is needed. Coupled to this advice, one always finds mentioned the need for strong leadership. People who are left to drift their own ways soon drift apart. A chicken without its head will not run a straight line. A typical example was the unfortunate Icarian community, whose president was not free even to buy a sack of wheat without the specific consent of the whole community. Even people with the best of intentions require coordination in a group endeavor.

Communities that have failed have done so, finally, because they lacked a clearly defined sense of purpose. A mere wish for economic stability does not seem to have been enough of a motive to inspire people to stick together. It is no accident that, of the successful ventures, nearly all have been religious.

How, then, might the pitfalls we have outlined be avoided?

First, let us not expect miracles. It is enough if a new way of life be *better* than the old. It is too much to ask that it also be perfect.

Policies pertaining to the acceptance of applicants are important. One carping fault-finder in a community can undermine the morale of many well-intentioned people. It would be wise; especially in a new community, to take care that only harmonious persons be admitted.

Again, there should be some system, some rules, but not with a view to creating goodness in people. One's vital concern should be for people as individuals, not as parts of a system. The system is needed only to coordinate the life of the community, not to be its salvation.

And let us not expect people to embrace a way of life too radically different from that to which they are now accustomed. This caution is important especially from the standpoint of enforcing "togetherness." A community of like minds cannot be forged on the strength of a theory. People must grow naturally to a sense of unity. The safest course for any new community would be to allow each person the freedom to meet others on his own terms.

And then, for a community to be intentional there must be *some* leadership. But a good leader will not be a dictator. He will encourage initiative on the part of the members. He will place human values ahead of the system, and inspire people to self-unfoldment. The less tight-knit a community, the greater the chances of its having this type of a leader. But where people are expected to do everything in common, to be of one mind on every issue, to eat together, play together, work always together, frictions can quickly mount. A community that strives for such constant, intense "togetherness" will require miracles of leadership to survive.

Consider, however, another type of community: the normal village, where "togetherness" is not driven down people's throats. There, administration is easily kept to a minimum. Villages have endured, where close-knit communities, lacking a strong leadership, have disintegrated.

The obvious solution, if one does not favor a dictatorship, is simply not to demand from people a constant togetherness, and hence a measure of unanimity, for which they are not prepared. The leadership of a community might then be strong, but not fussy. People would be given the freedom to grow, but would be given at the same time enough of a sense of common direction to help them to grow together, not apart.

A safe beginning, it seems to me, would be to heed well the fact that most successful colonies have been religiously oriented. If the idea of "world brotherhood colonies" is to spread, it would be well for at least the initial experiments not to be planned without including this (so far) all but essential ingredient.

But a religious orientation need not imply sectarianism. The pure essence of religion is its emphasis on an *inner* life. It is not because of religious fanaticism that communities have held together, but because the inner life developed in each member by his faith has given him a peace to smile away petty annoyances, a flexibility to meet his neighbor part way on disagreements, a freedom to enjoy things without attachment. In the sense of emphasizing this inner awareness, no community can afford to be lax. It is to make possible such an inner life that cooperative communities are needed in the first place.

Chapter Five

HOW TO BEGIN

I read in a local newspaper recently about someone who has been trying to start an ideal community, complete with progressive university, laboratories, concert halls – in short, all the social amenities, styled in impeccable architectural taste. He is trying to raise two and a half billion dollars for this dream-venture.

Others I have heard of, wealthy men, who have bought land with the intention of developing it for the future enjoyment of many people. Theirs are charitable ventures, from which others will benefit with a minimum of personal responsibility of their own.

What of the first venture? Two and one-half billion dollars is hardly a pittance! Anyone with such an impractical scheme would be lucky to raise two and a half thousand. No one wants to sail his money on the North Wind. But this example is worthy of notice, for people too often imagine that huge sums are required before a worthy project can be started and people brought together to work on it. The very opposite is true: people, by working together, produce wealth. Many great ventures have started on a shoestring. It is better to make a beginning with little than to spend years waiting for the skies to rain gold.

As for the charity of the wealthy man, he is at least in a position to make a beginning. But the willingness of people to accept his patronage without personal responsibility would spell sure death to any community. Even if people did work under such a scheme, what would their motive be? Gratitude? There is a point beyond which gratitude can become another word for slavery. No, it is better for people to own their own venture, and to work for it, knowing that in so doing they are working for themselves.

It is not difficult nowadays for a person to save $1,000 – certainly not where the incentive is present. A hundred people each saving $1,000 would have $100,000 – enough to make a very good beginning.

But there are ways to convert good intentions into reality. Consider one suggestion: Institute a "crash program" for several months. People can save considerably more than usual if they adopt the cooperative principle from the start, pooling their resources. Young people, especially, would find it easy to adapt themselves to such a scheme.

They could plan to share their meals in common. Meals for this period could be simplified. Cooking for many would greatly reduce costs and labor. A set fee could be paid by each participant for the three or four months. Cooking could either be done by rotation on a voluntary basis, or paid for, the cooks raising their own $1,000 through their work in the kitchen. Whatever money is left over could be used to buy grain for later use by the community.

Housing accommodations could be temporarily shared. To share one's room or apartment with others may not appeal to some people, but for three or four months it should be no great sacrifice for anyone.

It is not difficult in the cities nowadays to make $400 a month. If out of this amount $30 went towards food, and another $30 towards lodging, $300 a month could be saved easily toward the needed $1,000.

If this plan were not adopted, a regular weekly or monthly payment of $20 towards membership in the cooperative might ensure a more rapid saving than hording the money oneself against the day when this sum reaches the final $1,000 figure. ($300 in the bank, and a Sears Roebuck catalog on one's desk, can perform magic vanishing acts!)

Assuming that a substantial sum has been gathered, how then to proceed?

A good rule, based on the experience of other communities in the past, is: Don't borrow. Save money initially, if you have to, but remember that the community's income will be uncertain to begin with. The members may have to content themselves with eating only what they can grow. The burden of indebtedness at this early stage could be intolerable.

It would be wise not to buy land too far away from already developed areas. The community will need income, and will depend on its contacts with society at large to obtain it. It might even be wise not to settle too far away from the members' original home. San Francisco residents, for example, would find land cheaper in Oregon than in their own area, but – assuming that they need to begin the development on a part-time basis – it would also be more difficult for them to visit Oregon regularly. Worse still, the greater distance would greatly reduce the chances of drawing new recruits from their present circle of acquaintances. Most people would want to see the place before agreeing to live in it. Willing workers will be the community's greatest source of wealth. Why jeopardize that source by an initial saving, at the cost of continued accessibility?

If possible, land should be bought in sufficient quantity to permit future expansion, or in an area which holds a promise of future land acquisition. But such land is not always easy to find, and a reasonable alternative seems worth consideration: if the community flourishes, and succeeds in winning the friendship of the surrounding communities by being first a friend to them, it is at least conceivable that some of the neighbors will in time see the advantage to themselves of joining the community, and of adding their land to the whole.

Although a new cooperative community will not face the hardships of a single couple starting out on their own in the woods, the standard of living will certainly not compare with that which most of the members have known in the city. The first stages of community life will have to be for people with a pioneering spirit. Newcomers should be prepared in advance for a life of unaccustomed simplicity.

The labor of years will bring wealth. But need an exaggerated simplicity to begin with be a burden? Surely not! For anyone who knows to its heart the bondage of big city living, a simple life can only mean release from burdensome non-essentials for things more important to one's happiness.

As much as possible of the community's initial capital should be kept free for investment in various profitable ventures. The first residents may be content for some time to live in tents. A practical, and more comfortable, alternative would be the Navajo Indian *hogan*: Secondhand beams can be bought inexpensively, arranged in a large circular pattern, narrowed slowly to form a rounded roof with an opening in the center, then covered with plastic and chicken wiring, then with adobe. A movable plastic dome can be put over the opening at the top. For $100, perhaps less, one can have a remarkably roomy, comfortable, well-insulated home!

Crops should be planted as early as possible. If the community is not so fortunate as to have a farming expert among its members, those in charge of the farming should have the soil tested to ascertain its quality, and get advice on how to improve it if necessary. It would be wise to plan the crops for at least two years in advance.

One advantage of eating one's own produce will be readily appreciated by anyone who has had a chance to dine on a farm. Really fresh fruits and vegetables are a delight simply unknown to those who must eat their food hours, even days, after it has been picked.

It would be paradoxical for a community to embrace country life, and then to ignore the possibilities it provides for an improved diet. Almost nowhere in the cities can one find fruits and vegetables that have not been sprayed with pesticides, or treated with chemicals to make them grow larger and look better – all for the sake, not of health to the consumer, but of greater profits to the seller. Much has been written on the subject of pesticides and of chemical farming – enough to convince any thoughtful person to want his food unsprayed, and organically grown.

As insurance against future crop failures, the community should plan from the start to gather and store large supplies of whole grain, split peas, lentils, and other non-perishable foods.

One of the most expensive, and least healthful, items in the average food budget is meat. A community will be fortunate if it can agree to be vegetarian, at least as far as its own production and official consumption are concerned (leaving room, that is, for the individual who craves meat enough to buy it on the outside). Reasons for a meatless diet are given in some detail in my book, *Yoga Postures for Self-Awareness.*

A community may be surprised to discover how little money it actually requires for food. In 1950, I ate for some months on $7.50 a month, buying all my food at the grocery store. In 1960 I mentioned this feat to some friends. (They had been exclaiming on the high price of food).

"Oh, but in *1950* everything was different!" they assured me.

Perhaps so. But in 1963 I kept a similar budget for three months. Actually, it came to $10 a month, but roughly $2.50 of this amount went for desserts and other non-essentials. All I did was omit from my diet the more expensive items: meat (which I have not eaten now for almost twenty years), eggs, bread, butter, milk. Instead of bread, I ground my own flour and made an unleavened flat bread, like a tortilla. Frying this "chappati" (as it is called in India) in oil, I needed no butter. I trained my palate to like powered milk, which costs only a third as much as regular milk. I sprouted alfalfa seeds, ate nuts, fruits, and vegetables, made an occasional thick curried soup, or *daal*, of split peas or lentils. Raw fruits and vegetables gave me a maximum of nourishment in a minimum of bulk.

"The fruit of luxury," Thoreau wrote, "is luxury." The fruits of simple living are peace, happiness, and freedom. For many people, it would be no deprivation at all to live without modern conveniences, perhaps with gas lights, and with wood or oil stoves, and no telephone or television!

There is a story of an American Indian who supported his family by tilling a little plot of soil less than an acre in size. He was befriended by a neighbor, a wealthy white farmer. This man, pitying his poor friend for his meager subsistence, offered him several acres of adjoining land as a gift.

"You are kind," answered the Indian. "But see: The land I have is quite enough for our needs. If I had more to till, when would I find time for singing?"

If men would only simplify their needs, how much time might they not find to sing!

Chapter Six

COMMUNAL ECONOMICS

A vital question facing the cooperative society is that of the apportionment of wealth. The classical plan, dating as far back as apostolic days, has been for the members to own all things in common. Under this system, the individual has the use of whatever he receives from the community, but he may not consider it his personal property. In return for his work, he receives everything free of charge.

In a monastic community this scheme is perhaps right and just. Freedom from attachment to money and property, after all, is desirable in a person whose life is devoted to the spiritual search. But where families are concerned, I think this system is too restrictive, too much out of keeping with the consciousness of our age, and quite possibly tyrannical. It is also a real obstacle to the development of the community's economy.

The great problem with total communal ownership is that it increases the need for communal discipline. People who receive everything without paying for it must be induced somehow to work for what they get. Without the motive of personal profit, the only solution, if the community is to be productive at all, is to stress either group "spirit," or the beauty of holy obedience.

Advantage is too often taken of the resident's good will. He comes for a life of peace, and in the name of group spirit finds himself launched on all sorts of glorious projects: the construction of a new library, a hospital, a recreation center – and not just any kind of buildings, but, for the sake of the community's good name, the best imaginable. A community I know in India, seized with this noble motive, has devoted decades to building a temple that is intended to become more beautiful than the Taj Mahal. To what purpose?

If people were all highly spiritual, there would be no need to regiment them to be sure that they work, nor would there be any danger lest zealous leaders regiment them so much that they *over*-work. In fact, according to certain scriptures, if all people were truly spiritual they would receive the fruits of labor without working at all. But we are not living in such a spiritual age.

It is not surprising that, in Russia, where only 3% of the cultivated land is privately owned, this tiny portion supplies fully half of all the nation's meat, milk, and green vegetables. The early American colonies had a similar experience. Most people need to feel that they are working for themselves. They may actually be doing so just as much in a totally communistic society, but their vision is seldom broad enough clearly to grasp the fact.

Nor, it must be added, is the vision of communism's leaders any clearer. These persons tend in most cases to accept the worker's contribution as a matter of course, while remaining painfully conscious of the fact that, in addition to the burden of supervising his work, they must also feed, clothe, house, and entertain him. Small wonder that the benefits with which they supply him tend to be minimal and drab. And small wonder that he is treated to harsh discipline, and told that he must obey always and never think of himself and of his personal needs.

And if, in the case of a small communistic society, a member ever should leave, what will his recompense be? He will very likely be told that his stay there was permitted as a favor to him, that the community owes him nothing, save, perhaps, a reprimand for his ingratitude. After that, he may be given a pittance, out of "charity."

Thus it is – final indignity! – that many a monk or nun, and many a member of a completely communal society, has stayed on in the community not out of high ideals, but out of sheer economic need, passing his latter days in frustration, infecting others with his fits of irrational temper and his jealous pride of seniority. It is a situation comparable to that in *No Exit*, that thoroughly depressing play by Jean-Paul Sartre.

No, the soundest course, it seems to me, would be to follow the pattern to which people are in any case accustomed: Let them work for wages, and in turn pay for what they receive. Let them save what they like for the future. The simplest management is simply to give people the incentive to manage themselves. When they must look out for their own needs, they will bestir themselves well enough to produce.

We find in this proposed method another advantage: In the usual communistic community, the tendency is, as we have seen, to force people to overwork. If, however, a man must pay for everything he gets, it will be for him to decide how much income he really needs, and how many hours a week, in consequence, he must work. Under this system, if he wants to devote hours every day to painting or to meditating, he will more probably have the free time to do so.

The difference between the economic system here proposed and a normal system of free enterprise is that here the member remains, as in any cooperative, a part owner of the community. Whether in higher wages, discounts, stock dividends, or special benefits, he receives his share of the community's prosperity. It is up to him, by the contribution of his labor, to increase that prosperity or to keep it lower.

Specifically, the system recommended here might be described as follows:

Wages may be paid according to the community's work needs. To ensure that all work is done, the less popular jobs could pay better. People would be paid by the hour or by the job performed (depending on the type of work involved). Wherever possible, they themselves would decide how many hours they would work. But where other people were involved in a project, their decision would have to be submitted long enough in advance not to disrupt the whole work.

As a matter of fact, here at Ananda we have, so far at least, accepted as the simplest method the one for which our Western upbringing has best prepared us: Enterprising members have formed their own industries, and employ other members at whatever wages they can afford to pay. There is some talk among these owners of turning their businesses over to the central management of the community as a whole. So far, however, the persons most responsible for the community's finances have resisted such centralization as unwieldy, and quite possibly as detrimental to individual initiative.

Artists and artisans, selling their work through the community, would give the community the normal dealer's or agent's commission. Writers and others selling their works on the outside might be expected to pay the community a percentage of their royalties, for their work would be, in a sense, not their product alone, but would have been made possible by the very fact of the community's existence.

In addition to wages, a worker might be given a corresponding number of labor credits: one for each dollar that he earned as a direct result of labor for the community. The number of labor credits would determine, at the end of the year, his share in the community's prosperity. It must be added, however, that at Ananda we have not adopted this system. We consider it too cumbersome for our limited bookeeping.

To prevent anyone with sufficient wealth from controlling the community, the normal practice of cooperatives should be followed: Each member should have only one vote, regardless of how much money he puts into the community. For full voting membership, however, a person must make a minimum investment. At Ananda we have set the membership fee at $1,000 for single persons, and $1,500 for married couples.

Chapter Seven

COMMUNALISM VS. PRIVACY

Most spokesmen for the idea of cooperative communities have made it a point to emphasize the economy involved in feeding and housing everyone communally. B. F. Skinner wrote, in *Walden Two*, that if it were not for such communal facilities, "We should be occupying some two hundred and fifty dwelling houses and working in a hundred offices, shops, stores, and warehouses. It's an enormous simplification and a great saving of time and money."

But life offers many other satisfactions besides those that may be gleefully relished in saving time and money. I myself, when leaving my San Francisco apartment on an errand, used often to go out of my way to drive through Golden Gate Park. It may have been a waste in terms of time and gasoline, but the gain to my spirit was worth more to me.

No, to say that people *must* live together for any theoretical reason would be a mistake, as indeed it would also be to say they *must* live alone. For many an individual, a house and a garden of his own epitomizes the "good life."

Granted, a completely communal life *would* be economical. Shared facilities should certainly be provided for those people who prefer them. But anyone who would rather live in his own home should be given the freedom to do so. If he wishes to eat there, too, that should be his concern. If, on the other hand, he prefers the ease and economy of eating with others, there is no reason why there should not be a communal dining room where he can join them. A cohesive spirit should develop in a natural way, and not because of some theory wielded over the heads of the residents like a sledge hammer.

While members of the community should be granted a right to their own homes, however, newcomers might well be required for the first year to live communally. Objectionable characteristics would be more quickly observable. For the welfare of the community, only persons of reasonably harmonious disposition should be admitted to full residency.

A limit should be placed, however, on the amount of land any individual is allowed. A person or a family who live separately should be allowed only as much as they require for their building, with a small garden besides as a protection of their privacy.

Houses might all be built according to an accepted type. The heterogeneous impression given by most American cities is due largely to the confusion of their architectural styles. And the planning of the community's housing should be made with a view to future growth – an obvious point except for one observation: I believe that the problem, in time, will be one of too many people rather than too few. If the signs have been read correctly, we have entered a period in history when thousands will be drawn to this communal way of life. Paramahansa Yogananda wrote in terms of hundreds, even thousands, joining a single community. An *intentional* community of thousands, while almost certainly unacceptable to most people interested in communities today, would still be immensely preferable to the confusion of cross-currents that exists in the large cities.

A *Self-realization* community would probably elect to divide, however, long before it reached such a huge population. One or two hundred residents, including children, would probably be the preferred maximum. An eventual division should indeed be anticipated and desired from the start. Better many small communities in different parts of the country, where local people can visit them and observe this new way of life, than one large community in a single place, knowable to most people only through hearsay. Better in any case a small community. Excessive size will deprive it of much of its original charm.

Let us consider, then, the case of an eventual division. The "colonists," as we might call them, might be given their share out of the funds of the parent community, and perhaps also a loan without interest, and sent off on their own to found, not a branch, but another autonomous body. For no community of this nature can be guided practically from a distance. A new community might be under the "wing" of the parent for a time, but it must strive at the earliest possible opportunity to become independent.

In short, the motive spirit behind each community as a whole should be the same as that which would attract the individual to it: *Self-realization.*

And the spirit prevailing between the separate colonies should be the same as that which prevails within them between their individual members: co-operation.

Chapter Eight

EDUCATION

"As the twig inclineth, so doth the tree grow."

Education plays a vital role in any community. A cooperative community represents not only new opportunities for better living, but also a new outlook on life, one that can be developed most easily in children. But if the children are sent off to neighboring schools, the competitive spirit that is encouraged there will not advance their understanding of cooperation. Children are more inclined to imitate than to think for themselves.

The community should strive, then, as early as possible to build schools of its own – institutions where children can be taught how to *live*, not only how to add and subtract and recite from a catalogue of dry facts.

I have many friends in the teaching profession. It is surprising how many of them grumble at the public school system. Their chief complaint is that they have so little opportunity to be creative. The greater the size of any institution, the greater the need for imposing uniformity on its members. Eccentricity is anathema to the established order.

In a small cooperative school, however, there would be opportunity for endless creativity. Teaching could be a constant experiment with new and better ways of imparting knowledge and understanding.

With an attractive approach to education, there is no reason why group training of a sort should not begin early in life, with specially trained "baby sitters." Modern social conditioning may influence people to feel that a mother ought to be with her children all the time. But why? When she is busy with her housework she is not in any case free to play with them; they are merely in her way. The time that she can actually devote to them, after her housework is finished, may be marred by the memory of a long day of scoldings and spankings.

My own early years were spent in Rumania, where my father worked as an oil geologist. Living there, my parents, as Americans, were able to afford a nurse. I have often heard them remark that the freedom they had, because of her, made it possible for them to enjoy us far more than they would have done otherwise. And, looking at the matter from our standpoint as children, I can truthfully say that it would be difficult to imagine a happier childhood, or a greater feeling of love and respect than we felt for our parents.

But communal schooling from an early age will also help to accomplish something for which every wise parent should strive: It will expand the child's sense of identity. The "us four and no more" attitude is selfish and blinding. One of the very purposes of a cooperative community must be to expand people's sympathies.

To consider again my own childhood, ours also was a quasi communal life – a number of families fenced in next to a large oil refinery, named, "Teleajen." We each gave special affection to our own parents, but we addressed all the other adults affectionately as "Uncle" and "Auntie."

Why not? The community should be the child's expanded family. Thus, one may well come in time to know all men as his brothers.

It is doubtful whether competitive games and sports can be banned without washing much of the color out of a child's life. But the emphasis, certainly, should be on games in which the child can concentrate on improving his own skills rather than on beating down an opponent.

Grading, similarly, should be done as much as possible on a basis of the teacher's estimate of the child's potential rather than on a scale of comparison with other students. Comparison of one's own mental development with that of anyone else is seldom constructive. (The teacher might, however, assign an objective grade that would be kept in the student's file for future college entrance requirements.)

Every child should be encouraged to develop according to his own natural bent. Each should select, as a hobby, some special interest or trade. In this field he would receive personal training. (Each member of the community, in fact, should develop some handicraft that can be turned to the benefit of the community.)

One of the curses of the average school system is the limit it places on creativity. It is no accident that many a creative genius has left his formal education unfinished. For the best way to receive good grades in school is to anticipate the teacher's interests. Girls generally do better than boys simply because they are more skilled in the art of diplomacy. But the trend ought to be just the reverse: It is the teacher who should do his best to find and develop the student's interests.

The chief obstacle to his doing so, usually, is that he has a text book to follow. As much as possible, in the community's school, teaching should be done from life itself, not from the fixed and brittle dogmas of a book.

Each student should be taught also the basic arts of living: how to concentrate, the beauty of kindness and cooperation, how to overcome fear, anger, and jealousy, how to meditate and develop an inner life, how to appreciate the higher values in life. These are not matters for classroom pedagogy. They will require life situations and wise, personal guidance from the teachers. But they should be a vital part of any "how-to-live" school.

While teaching academic subjects, advantage should be taken of the natural tendency of children to hero worship. They could be introduced to the great men and women of history, not incidentally only, but as vitally connected with their discoveries and achievements. "A nation is known," Dr. Radhakrishnan, India's Vice President, once remarked to me, "by the men and women it looks upon as great." By the same token, an emphasis on the example of certain great persons can help a child to develop definite ideals. For a child thinks more easily in terms of persons than of principles.

But to suspend a great figure in midair over the barren plains of a vanished era would not be instructive enough. His culture, the general interests of the people of his time, a consideration of the similarities between that age and our own – all these would help in the presentation of academic facts and principles. In this connection, a pet educational theory of my own has long been to steep the student completely in one subject at a time, instead of obliging him to jump back and forth between completely unrelated fields: French, geometry, American history, physics. I remember years ago taking up a study of the fine points of English grammar. For two weeks I did nothing else. In school, a year of scattered classes and homework assignments would have been needed to cover the same ground, and I would have forgotten most of what I had learned within a month after the final exam. Concentration it is that deepens the memory impressions in the brain. The information I absorbed in two weeks of *concentrated* study has remained with me to this day.

If a student could study one subject at a time for periods of, let us say, one month, and vary his mental fare by excursions into *related* fields, I venture to say that he would learn far more, and become far more interested in the process. A study of Algebra, for example, could involve him also in a study of the Arabs, who brought this ancient science from India. It could touch on the uses of symbolic thinking in real life situations. It could cover the adventure of modern science, and the great scientists who brought the scientific revolution to pass.

And what matter if, in the course of a year, the same subjects be touched on more than once? Approached several times in relation to different fields of interest, they should yield new information and wisdom every time.

I do not say that any of the above points is necessary for the development of education in a cooperative community. All of them illustrate, however, an essential feature of any such education: that it be kept free for experimentation.

Chapter Nine

GOVERNMENT

Many utopian writers have given themselves up to dreams of a society without a government. What they have envisioned is a nation in a state of perfect equilibrium, where each person knows his own place. The old Greek, Heraclitus, had an answer for this type of thinking. "All," he said, "is flux." Living organisms achieve perfect equilibrium only in death. Otherwise, all things move. Death itself is only life's way of stepping aside to make way for new living forms.

No, some form of government will always be necessary, and the successes and failures of countless communities suggest that it had better be a strong government. But leadership can be strong without being dictatorial. A dictatorship would be far from the spirit of a *cooperative* community. Granting a government the power to act as and when necessary, the best government will still be that which, as Thoreau put it, rules the least, which encourages personal initiative and responsibility, and which legislates in matters of communal *convenience* rather than of personal outlook and growth.

The fact that man has experimented with so many different types of government suggests that the perfect system still remains to be found. In fact, as I have already pointed out elsewhere, no system can be any better than the people whose lives it directs. There can be no "perfect" system, for its members will always be the determining factor in its performance. A system can *facilitate* the expression of goodness in people; it cannot *create* goodness. Let us, then, look for an efficient government, but not for a perfect one.

Ananda Cooperative Community offers one possible system of communal government. Here at Ananda we have sought not only efficiency, but *simplicity*, in the management of our affairs. Our Board of Directors, which (to avoid the usual mental association of bosses and underlings) we prefer to call the Planning Board, is elected annually by resident members who have lived here for more than one year. This Planning Board is answerable to the general membership, in which the over-all governing power actually resides.

The officers, elected by the Planning Board from among its own members, consist of a Spiritual Director (a position comparable to that of president), a General Manager (whose position corresponds to that of vice president), a Secretary, and a Treasurer.

The Spiritual Director might, in less explicitly spiritual communities, be the person responsible for guiding the members in their own chosen ideals, whatever these might be. Idealism, not expediency, should be the final arbiter in all cooperative community affairs. I feel that it is important, therefore, that this presiding officer not be directly involved in practical community management. At Ananda, this officer's primary concern is the community's spiritual welfare. His duty is to coordinate the secular with the spiritual activities of the community, and, by not becoming too involved in secular matters, to preserve an over-all view which might otherwise be lost in the pressures of the moment.

The actual management of day-to-day matters at Ananda is the duty of the General Manager. His function is similar in most respects to that of the manager of a business corporation, with the main exception that spiritual principles are the supreme arbiter of his activities, and that in such matters he confers with the Spiritual Director, as well as, of course, being subject to the supervisory control of the Planning Board.

I have outlined our government so far as if it were already an established legal fact, and not only a more or less informal custom. As a matter of fact we are still, as this sixth edition goes to press, only in the process of becoming legally incorporated. Further changes, at present unforeseen, may yet have to be made in our procedures. The following direct quotation from our prospective by-laws, then, should be taken as only provisional, though it is, I believe, a reasonable enough statement for any community to adopt.

"The Planning Board may appoint individual members of the community to be responsible, as the need arises, for other specific areas of community activity. Such specific areas might include the following, by way of illustration and example.

a. Director of Housing, Parks, and Community Lay-out.
b. Director of Farming and Industrial Planning.
c. Director of Entertainment, Recreation, and Cultural Expression.
d. Director of Public Relations and Instruction.
e. Director of Education and Admissions.

f. Director of Public Works.

"In order that Planning Board members be elected primarily on the basis of their spiritual dedication and *general* executive ability, rather than on a basis of specialized knowledge in any of the above fields, Directors shall not be elected to any of these posts as such, if it is created, but they may be appointed to it by the Board. Sub-committees of specialists can be formed subsequently, under the general coordination of one or another of the Board members."

In all cooperative communities, elections should be held without campaigning, and by secret ballot. Only voting members who are established residents of the community should be allowed to vote in elections of Board members and on other "in-community" matters. Members who are not established residents might, however, be invited to vote in matters pertaining to income and investment that, owing to the seriousness of their nature, are offered for the decision of the general membership.

Within the framework outlined above, every member should have the same voting power as any other.

It may be necessary for new communities to grow slowly even into such a simple governmental structure as I have outlined here. For if they plunge too hastily into a cloud of formalities, they may lose sight of the real reason for which they first got together.

Chapter Ten

RULES

Rules should be kept at a minimum. It is far better to establish general customs than hard and fast laws. "Too many rules," Yogananda said, "destroy an institution's spirit." Even if everyone follows a rule, the fact that it *is* a rule makes it fertile soil for gossip and suspicion. ("Did you hear that John *borrowed the garden hose* yesterday?" "Dear God, no!") It acts as a narrowing influence upon the mind, where simple customs might only help everyone to grow harmoniously. It is better, then, to deal as much as possible with individual cases as they arise, and as the circumstances dictate, without going on from there to establish a rule rigidly binding upon a majority who would never consider offending against it anyway.

Certain rules there will have to be, of course. It would be unfair to the newcomer to give him no clear sense of the direction in which the community is proceeding. It would also be difficult for the community to proceed smoothly toward its goals without some definite sense of what those goals are, and how best to reach them. In this respect, certainly, an *intentional* community must differ from the directionless hodgepodge that constitutes the average village.

The orientation of a Self-realization cooperative should be implicit in those very words: *Self-realization* is essentially an inward goal; *cooperative* implies a spirit of voluntary, rather than forced, cooperation of the members with one another. Both ideals – individual development and voluntary cooperation – imply a respect for one another's rights which leaves no room for egoistic individualism (the kind which is careless about imposing on the freedom of others). Remember, too, that in an intentional community individual development and voluntary cooporation are interactive principles. The member who develops himself inwardly is thereby helping to uplift the others as well. The member, on the other hand, who makes no effort to improve himself cannot validly claim that his indolence is no one's business but his own. His lack of effort is a detriment to the sincere efforts of others.

Proscriptive rules should be few. One such rule should definitely take into account the fact that every community so far that has permitted the use of drugs has soon drifted into a sense of communal irresponsibility, the sure precursor of communal disintegration.

It would be wise also to prohibit alcoholic beverages as a useless indulgence among people who are trying to live a better, healthier life.

Smoking might be discouraged without any actual rule being made against it. The members might simply be asked to abstain from smoking in public places, or wherever their smoking might affect others. At Ananda, where most of the members are vegetarian, the question of meat-eating also is treated in this way.

Here are a few suggestions, only, for basic rules that a community might do well to adopt.

1. No job shall be played up as more dignified

than any other.

2. No one may act in such a way as to harm another. (This rule might be interpreted subtly, as well as literally, for a negative personal example can, in certain cases, be as injurious to a community as actual physical violence.)

3. Voting must be considered a privilege, not a duty. No one should vote unless he has formed a definite opinion on the subject under consideration.

4. No hallucinogenic drugs or alcoholic beverages may be taken by any member of the community, on or off the community property.

Chapter Eleven

WHAT IS ANANDA?

The reader has already been informed that an actual experiment in cooperative living, known as Ananda Cooperative Community, is being carried out by the author and some of his friends in the mountains of northern California on the basis of the ideas presented in this book. You may yourself have wondered more than once already, "Why go to all the trouble of starting something myself, when there is a community already flourishing that I might join?"

As a matter of fact, we might be happy if you reached this conclusion. But please bear in mind that communities, like people, develop distinct characters of their own. To live in a place with a different character from yours might impede your development, even though its final goals and yours be the same. Many are the roads to truth, and many and varied are the possible applications of broad principles such as those which have been outlined in these pages.

Ananda presents only one such application. Not everyone who reads this book and is attracted by its ideas will feel similarly attracted to the community that I have founded. This is, I believe, quite as it should be. The world would be a very dull place indeed if all men liked and did the same things. The most universal principles must lose some of their universality in actual application, for every such application can be nothing but a limited *example* of the principle itself. Other, and perhaps very different, applications might exemplify it just as truly.

Ananda is a yoga-oriented community. It is dedicated to the search for God and to serving Him through hard, self-purifying work. Our members are disciples, or at least devotees, of Paramahansa Yogananda and of his line of Gurus. Most of them are members also of Self-Realization Fellowship, the organization which Yogananda started in this country in 1920. Ananda is not, however, formally affiliated with that or with any other organization.

When Paramahansa Yogananda, during his public lectures in the last years of his life, urged his listeners to band together into "world brotherhood colonies," the general expectation was that his own organization would take the first steps towards forming such a community. But Yogananda was urging his listeners *themselves* to take the initiative. His organization had, and is likely to continue to have, more than it can do already to serve the spiritual demands that are placed upon it by a world-wide and growing interest in yoga. For a community to be successful it is vitally necessary in any case that it run itself; it cannot be supervised effectively from a distance. Its problems will be immediate; they can be solved only by painstaking experiment, not by the remote directives of some larger, but less directly involved, institution.

Ananda is, therefore, a completely autonomous body.

We are not sectarian, but we find it helpful in our

own home environment for our members to be following the same path together.

And what is this path? A few of its highlights are:

A belief in the essential oneness of all religions, and a universal respect for their teachings.

A belief in the value of meditation, and in the spiritual life as the summum bonum of human existence.

Respect for the great saints of all religions, who have fulfilled in their own lives the highest spiritual teachings.

A belief that it is insufficient merely to believe – that spiritual truths must be practiced and *experienced* in one's own life, through meditation.

Part II of this book presents the story of our beginnings. The fact that Ananda has been started and is, so far at least, remarkably successful, should give hope to others who have wanted to found similar communities, but who have feared that after all the whole idea, in this age of business mergers and sprawling urban communities, might prove impracticable.

Some people would rather join an already-working venture. Others prefer the challenge of starting something themselves. If you do start a cooperative community, I hope you will contact us. We may still be too young ourselves to offer you very much assistance or advice, but it would be good in any case for the cooperative communities in America to become a sort of loose-knit spiritual brotherhood – not formally bound together, but extending to one another that spirit of cooperation which is the basic feature of the cooperative way of life.

PART II

Chapter One

THE EARLY YEARS

Ananda Cooperative Community and Ananda Meditation Retreat are the result of years of intensive work, the cooperation of many friends, faith, and an almost continuous series of miracles.

It all started many more than nine years ago, really, with the study and dreams described in the Introduction to this book. But its more active beginnings date back to 1962. Paradoxically, they first took the form of a search for a place of personal retreat and seclusion for myself.

The religious organization to which I had belonged for fourteen years, and of which I was then the first vice president, dismissed me quite suddenly on July 28, 1962. My belief in decentralization, wherever possible, as a vital factor in spreading the work had brought me under suspicion of being a potential schismatic.

New doors, as it happened, were being held open for me, but at that time I could see only that every familiar door had been closed. My one desire now was to find a place where I might remain quiet and alone, to pray deeply for new directions.

As everyone knows, it takes money to live in this

world. I was offered a post teaching yoga at the American Academy of Asian Studies, in San Francisco, and could not afford to turn it down. Later, I taught at the Cultural Integration Fellowship, also in San Francisco. Gradually, the expense of city living forced me to teach other classes also, on my own. And thus my longing for seclusion, which never left me, was obliged patiently to await its appointed hour.

In the meantime, the number of my new friends was growing steadily.

Through the years between 1962 and 1967, I sought repeatedly for a place of retreat: up and down the coast of northern California, in the Sierra Nevada, in Arizona. I even made a fruitless journey to Arkansas, and looked at land on the coast of Mexico. I had little money, and did not want to live on someone else's property as a guest. Yet I believed that, if the place presented itself, the means to acquire it would be found also.

The longer I waited, however, the more friends I acquired through my lectures and yoga classes. The thought of seeking a spiritual retreat for myself alone came into increasing conflict with my wish to be of spiritual service to those who depended on me. And so it was that the thought of forming a cooperative community stole up on me once again, as if by a back door. While half of my mind was thinking of finding a place of personal privacy and seclusion, the other half was thinking more and more of a place where others, too, might be able to live a spiritual life together.

All the currents in my life, including especially those since July, 1962, in one way or another influenced the formation and development of Ananda Cooperative Community, and helped to determine its special character. Looking back now, I see a pattern in the apparent self-contradiction of wanting a place for seclusion, and at the same time a place where I might build a community. Often, I believe, we are led as it were unconsciously in the direction in which we are meant to go. Even my sudden, and at that time (to me) tragic, severance from the organization to which I had dedicated my life proved at last and in many ways a blessing. At least I can say that if it had not occurred, this book would not have been written, and Ananda would have remained but a dream.

Chapter Two

LAND HO!

It was January, 1967. I had not yet found the land I wanted, but the income for it was suddenly beginning to materialize. The Peace Corps had offered me a well-paying job for a semester at the University of California at Davis. (I was to teach a group of volunteers all about Indian culture and civilization, but my approach began with Indian philosophy, and this proved too much for them. They wanted, they said, to learn about *India*, not about Indian philosophy. So I brought in outside teachers to tell them about five-year plans, and – on their insistence – about the negro question in America.) In addition, I had begun charging for my yoga classes – reluctantly at first, because I look upon teaching as a form of service, and had therefore been simply letting people donate as they could, or as they chose. I had come to find, however, that for many students the absence of a fee tends to make their attendance and personal practice more or less casual. At last I was persuaded to set a fee, though at the same time I determined not to exclude sincere-seeming students who could not afford to pay it. The plan worked well: There was a remarkable increase in the seriousness of the students, and a sudden spurt also in my income. I had a feeling that I would soon be needing this extra money.

I was right. Until this time, I had been content to live marginally, barely raising the money each month to pay the rent on my apartment. But the time was fast approaching when I would take the first definite steps toward developing what was to become known as Ananda.

The income I derived from the Peace Corps job enabled me to publish my first books: *Yours—the Universe!*, *Yoga Postures for Self-Awareness*, and *The Book of Bhrigu* (a report on an ancient Indian book of prophecy). With these publications I set up the first business by which I hoped the cooperative community, once I had founded it, would support itself.

Jeannie Campbell, the receptionist and general secretary for the print shop where two of these books were being printed, was a devout Zen Buddhist. We had many lively discussions on the differences between zen and yoga. She also gave me a running description of the development of Tassajara, a Zen Buddhist retreat that was being built in the mountains near Carmel, California, and a place with which she was closely connected.

During the course of one of these conversations, I told her of my wish to find some land for a retreat of my own.

"Say," she cried, "why don't you contact Dick Baker? He's the president of the Zen Center here in San Francisco, and he's in charge of building Tassajara. If anyone would know about available land, he would."

I dutifully jotted his name down, but never got around to phoning him. In my long experience of "leads" that had led nowhere, this one seemed simply another improbability.

A week or two later, however, I was in a small shop in San Francisco, and was obliged to wait while another customer was being served. This person was speaking of some land that he and some friends were thinking of buying for a retreat. Unable to resist the entree, I mentioned that I was looking for something similar myself. During the course of a still-casual conversation, he pulled out a map of his proposed property and spread it out on a table, adding that he still needed a few people to buy into the property with him.

Had this looked like an ordinary real estate deal, I might not have been quite so intrigued, but he wanted the land for a spiritual retreat. This was definitely intriguing. As a person, too, I found him attractive. "What is your name?" I asked.

"Dick Baker."

The very person Jeannie had urged me to look up! As Dick explained it to me later, when the appeal went out to raise the money for the purchase of Tassajara, the sum involved was so high that it drew a number of alternate offers from friends and sympathizers. These persons wrote to say, in effect, "If you find that you can't raise that much money, I have some land that I'd be willing to sell you at a very low price because of the spiritual purpose involved."

Partly to check out possible alternatives to Tassajara, and partly because he also wanted a place of retreat for himself and his family, Dick Baker had visited all of the proposed places. Of them all, his favorite was a tract of 172 acres in the foothills of the Sierra Nevada, near Nevada City, California. It was only $250 an acre – inexpensive for California, in fact only half the usual price of land even in this remote area. But it was more money than Dick personally could afford. He decided, therefore, to try to get six of his friends to purchase the land with him, each of them receiving twenty-four acres. Somehow the idea, and Dick Baker himself, felt completely "right" to me. I asked him if I might accompany him on his next trip up there. He said he was planning one in the early spring, and that he would be glad for me to come along.

When we went up, it was with two of his friends, Allen Ginsberg and Gary Snyder, both well-known poets, and both interested in buying twenty-four-acre parcels for themselves. A woman writer accompanied us, too; she was working on an article about Allen for *The New Yorker.*

Our trip took us far out into the countryside. The last three miles were dirt road, deeply rutted and barely passable after the winter rains. The altitude was 3,000 feet. The air was fresh. The property was rolling, wooded, serene, and gave onto several beautiful views of distant snow-capped mountains. I went off in one direction by myself. Gary went in another. We were "feeling" the land.

The impression came to me strongly that my Gurus had already blessed the particular section of the land to which I had felt drawn. It was an eastern exposure, and to me, as a yogi, especially attractive. Would the others want it too? If it came to a conflict of interests, I knew that, as the latecomer to the group, I was the last in line to choose.

But amazingly, each of us felt drawn to a different section of the property. I could not help feeling that it was for this place that God had made me wait all those years. At last my search was ended.

But I little knew what struggles had just begun!

When the weather is warm, I lead Sunday services out of doors at Ananda Meditation Retreat.

Chapter Three

MY FIRST NON-HOME

Somehow I find that I have always lived my life on two levels: a conscious level, on which I approach things according to my own personal inclinations; and another one, more dimly perceived, on which I seem to know how things are going to have to be whether I want them that way or not. My experience in being dismissed in 1962 came as a complete shock on one level; on the other, though no warning had been given, it was expected long in advance.

An example of this curious dual awareness concerns another case where one level pitted itself against the other. In the latter months of 1963 I was staying on a ranch in Arizona. At that time I was hoping that I might support myself by writing, and was determined if possible to avoid all public activity.

I received a letter in November from Dr. Haridas Chaudhuri, the founder-director of Cultural Integration Fellowship in San Francisco, inviting me to give a series of classes in his ashram that winter. I wrote back explaining my anxiety to stay out of the public eye. Yet I knew with a puzzling inner certainty that I would be not only teaching in his ashram that winter, but living in it.

I returned to the San Francisco Bay area to be with my parents for Christmas. Shortly afterward I was invited to attend a quiet Saturday evening dinner at which Dr. Chaudhuri and his wife also were guests. My scheduled departure for Arizona was only four days away. My inner certainty of an unscheduled change, however, had prevented me from even thinking about packing. At the end of the evening, the Chaudhuris bade me a safe journey. There was something about our parting that was unreal.

The next morning, in the middle of his Sunday sermon, Dr. Chaudhuri fell over with a heart attack and was rushed in a critical condition to the hospital. He had no one to take his place at the ashram. As his friend, I knew I had no choice but to offer my services during the long months it would take him to recuperate.

In a similar manner I knew, when I first bought the land for my retreat, that I would not be permitted to enjoy it until I had founded a community as well. I wanted in any case to share the retreat with a few others as temporary guests, or as permanent hermits. But the community that I felt I was being directed to form was a busy place for families with children, self-supportive industries – in short, a place such as I have described in the first part of this book.

What about my long-desired seclusion? The community, I decided, would have to wait. The retreat for others would have to wait. First I would have my own place. Everything else could develop gradually, if it was meant to, out of this first step. I should have listened to that soft inner whisper. It told me from the start that I had made the wrong choice, and that if the other ventures were to develop in the right way, I would have to think of myself last, not first.

"But all I want," I told myself, "is a place to seek God. What's so selfish about that?" If I'd waited for an answer, the rest of that year might have gone more smoothly for me.

As a structure for my home, I had decided if possible to build a dome. The idea had first come to me in India, in 1961. There I had planned to build a temple, and my meditations had suggested this type of structure to my mind as the most conducive to inner calmness and expansion. What I envisioned was a hemisphere coming down on all sides to about eye level – more or less like the inside of a planetarium. A flat ceiling, it seemed to me, had the psychological, perhaps even psychic, effect of pressing down on the head. An arched ceiling seemed to invite aspiration, but more in the form of external than of internal worship. The high domes that one finds in some temples around the world suggest a heavenly state far removed from any present human expectations. For meditation, with the inner peace that it brings to the soul even in the present life, the sort of dome I envisioned seemed ideal. It harmonized with nature herself, with her round "inverted bowl" of the sky. The human head, too, is a dome; perhaps the rays of energy going outward from the brain are echoed back most harmoniously from the inner surface of a similar structure. After returning from India I visited a planetarium, and was interested to discover that even with children squirming and giggling all around me, and while people were still entering and the lights were still on, a distinct impression of peace emanated from that interior.

I wanted, as I say, to construct a perfect dome. But inquiries convinced me that the cost would be prohibitive. One day, Karen Leffler, a student in one of my classes, introduced me to a concept that was new to me: the geodesic dome, an invention by Buckminster Fuller. For me, it was a compromise. His straight lines and flat planes produce a marvel of engineering, but esthetically they conflict with the roundness of a true hemisphere. Still, it was the closest thing to a possibility that I had come upon so far. I resolved to follow in the footsteps of Buckminster Fuller.

It was easier resolved than done. No one seemed to know the mathematical formula. One company that I found made domes, but were tool designers, not artists; their squat structures looked to me like toadstools out of a book of nursery rhymes. This, I decided, was just too much of a compromise.

At last Charles Tart, a professor at U.C. Davis, showed me a geodesic dome that he was constructing in his back yard. It was called a "sun dome." Inexpensive, beautiful in its simplicity, and easy for an amateur like me to construct, it offered me my first ray of real hope. I clutched it as eagerly (and as foolishly) as a drowning man would a straw.

Easy it may have been to construct, but building the platform, cutting the struts exactly to the required angles, assembling them into triangles, then covering them with plastic, required months of unceasing labor. After all my years of waiting, I was determined to build my retreat if possible this year.

No, Kriyananda, it was not to be. I got the dome up all right. The last triangle was about to go in, after which, supposedly, the dome would stand firm. But until it had been fully assembled, its strength was precarious.

Suddenly a strong gust of wind rushed up from the valley; the entire structure fell to the ground, a jumble of matchsticks and plastic.

Refusing to give up, I set out immediately to replace the broken pieces, reassembling all the triangles, and stapling them together with greater care than the first time. Weeks later, the new structure was up. It was, in all fairness, more beautiful than anything we have built since. Its delicate struts were an esthetic delight. But Keats was wrong: Beauty is not necessarily truth. The "sun dome" proved a snare and a delusion.

I did not realize that the planners had designed it to sit cozily in a fenced-in back yard, as Charlie Tart's was, well protected from strong winds, and preferably even from the mildest zephyr. Up on the hilltop at Ananda the late autumn winds can get up to sixty or seventy miles an hour. In the first storm we had, my beautiful dome-house simply disintegrated. I walked away from it without even looking back.

But after a few days I summoned the courage to try once again. This time, after re-cutting many more pieces and reassembling them, I screwed them all firmly together with large metal plates. This time, I was sure, no wind could possibly rip them apart.

The wind didn't have to. Alas, I knew nothing of its power to lift a hemisphere, similarly to the lift it exerts on the upper portion of the wing of an airplane. I returned to Ananda soon after I had put up my dome for the third time. I was eager, before winter descended in earnest, to get at least a little of that solitary meditation I had been planning for so long.

I arrived to find pieces of the dome draped artistically over the surrounding bushes. Worst of all, because this time the pieces had been screwed so firmly together, virtually every one of them was broken. There was nothing to do but recognize defeat, and accept it calmly. I sat down on the open platform, and, surprisingly perhaps, had a joyous meditation.

But to me it was a sign that I would not be able to have my own home until I had built a temple, and perhaps even a community, for the benefit of others.

Our recent geodesic domes, like this one, have been more successful.

Chapter Four

ANANDA MEDITATION RETREAT

My home-to-be had blown down for the third time. I found myself almost without funds. There was no choice for me but to go back to teaching classes again. This I did intensively, traveling to a different city every evening, determined now to raise the money necessary to build a retreat for others as well as for myself. And as long as I was putting forth so much energy, I decided if possible also to take the first steps toward building the cooperative community I had been contemplating.

To many people, my dream of starting a community, and at the same time of spending a long time in seclusion, must have seemed absurdly self-contradictory. But I knew now that it was not so much a question of what *I* wanted, but of what God wanted for me. And somehow an inner intuition assured me that the two things *would* be possible.

For nothing within me responded to the idea of *managing* a cooperative community. I knew that if I, as the founder, took up the task of administrating its affairs, and of personally guaranteeing its success, I would have to write off the next twenty-five years of my life to developing this project alone. My task, I felt, was rather to devote my energies, and such experience as I might be able to claim, to helping *others* to form a community. I might serve it thereafter, if the members so wished, as a spiritual director, but definitely not as a business manager. If I could adhere to the single role of spiritual counselor, it seemed to me that seclusion much of the time would actually help me in that work.

There was another factor influencing my decision to begin now, rather than later, to develop the community. It was the feeling, in a positive sense, that there might not be very much time left to get it going. When large masses of people speak of sensing an impending cataclysm, one cannot but feel that something serious may well be in the air. I was conscious also of my own corroborative feelings in the matter, and especially of the many dire warnings of my Guru.

A busy community of families, self-supportive industries, and crying babies would have ruined the meditative calm of the retreat. It would have betrayed not only my personal hopes, but also the condition on which Dick Baker had been kind enough to let me buy into the property. None of the others was planning to build there for at least two years, however. Nor did I see how, in my present role as a fund raiser, I could hope to get any seclusion sooner than that. A strong sense that the community was destined to be gave me confidence that, if we started it at the Retreat, it would soon be strong enough to move onto land of its own.

There was another factor influencing the direction of my thinking. Two twenty-four-acre parcels adjoining mine had not yet been sold. It was already late in January, 1968, and, according to our agreement with the sellers, if all seven of the parcels were not sold by April 1st of that year the entire sale would fall through. Dick was confident that he would find the extra buyers, but so far, in ten out of thirteen months, only we, the original four, had bought land there. I was not quite so confident that three more people would come forward in the remaining two months to save the situation.

I phoned Dick and told him that I might be able to buy the two parcels next to mine. "But please understand," I said, "that I would not buy this land only for my own retreat. For that, twenty-four acres are quite enough." I went on to describe my community idea, and to assure him that the use of these extra acres for that purpose would be only temporary. It was asking a lot of him to believe that I would really be in a position to move the community away in two or three years (I believe we set the maximum limit at five years), but he must have caught some of my conviction, for he agreed.

For years an old friend of mine, Oleta Burger, had been offering to give me money to help start a community. Repeatedly I had put her off, wanting to test the sincerity of her offer. I now told her that I thought the time was right, and asked if she was still interested. She was. In this way the two extra parcels at the Retreat were acquired, bringing our total number of acres to seventy-two.

Soon afterwards I called the first formal meeting to discuss plans for forming a cooperative community. I had planned to have only a few close friends and co-workers at this first meeting. Others, however, whom I hardly knew, but who claimed to be interested in the project, appeared also, uninvited. Their presence proved a mixed blessing.

"How do we know you're on the level?" one of them demanded.

"If you start something this big, you'll soon forget all about your ideal of serving people."

"I know a teacher from India who became involved in building a place similar to this. It took so much of his energy that he lost his inner peace, and today he's a MONSTER!"

"Think of it, everyone. If Kriyananda really wanted to draw us into this thing as partners, *why didn't he call this meeting sooner?*"

The only thing to do at this point was to serve tea and cookies.

But the meeting was not a total disaster. Realizing that by mere talk I would never be able to give people a clear picture of what I had in mind, I sat down at last with the gathered notes and reflections of many years, and wrote this book. After publishing it in loose-leaf form, and distributing it to all who expressed an interest in the idea, I decided to give everyone time to reflect on it before broaching the subject again.

My own enthusiasm had led me to expect a quick, positive response from anyone to whom I described my ideas. I had overlooked the many years it had taken me to grow into these ideas myself.

Many potentially interested persons, I now realized, needed not only enough time to reflect on these ideas, but also the reassurance of seeing something already solidly accomplished. It is one of the curious facts of human life that, for most ventures to be started, people are the prime necessity, but that, for most people to become involved at all, the venture itself must already be well under way.

No one, I decided, could accuse me of black motives if I built a meditation retreat. It was a project about which little theorizing was necessary, and it would attract active participation. Slowly, out of this group labor, the seeds were to sprout that would grow in time to become the cooperative community.

I had reached the conclusion, by means which the tactful reader will doubtless fail to recognize, that I was not cut out to be a carpenter. The worst of it was that none of my friends were carpenters, either. But by this time I was making a fair amount of money teaching classes. Some money was coming in also from generous friends. This income, plus some stocks that my father had given me over the years, totaled about sixteen thousand dollars – enough for me to think of hiring professional help.

I still wanted those geodesic domes. The only company that made them was still that one which manufactured pre-fabs vaguely reminiscent of toadstools. I bowed to the inevitable. At least these were something I could afford.

I found a carpenter who expressed confidence that he would be able to put up our buildings in two weeks. "Go ahead," I told him. Had I shared his experience in construction, I doubt that I would have shared his confidence.

The first thing the carpenter (now the foreman) wanted was a couple of professional helpers. A number of my friends worked with him, too, at greatly reduced wages, glad (I hope) of the chance to spend a summer out of doors in the woods. In these ways wages soared to $1,000 a week. But the worst news was still to come. After two weeks, around the middle of July, 1968, not even the foundations had been finished. In all, the project was to take two and a half months. Long before that time, I ran out of money.

No problem, I told myself. The bank would surely lend me what I needed.

But they wouldn't. Their reasoning went something like this: So I was making money by teaching yoga; so, maybe a few people were crazy enough to study this absurd "science," but after all, one can't fool all the people all of the time; the yoga fad was bound to pass, and, if one was to have any faith in human nature at all, one surely couldn't expect such madness to last out the year.

For me, their rejection was a major blow. We had a temple, a common dome (kitchen, dining room, and living room), bath house, office, and my home all under construction, and it was imperative that they be finished before the winter storms ruined them. But the next thing I knew, the foreman and one of his two professional helpers had walked off the job. The third carpenter remained loyal, but we still had bills outstanding that amounted to thousands of dollars. Only to complete the construction was to cost me at least another $12,000. I was just screwing up my courage to try to raise this amount when the local lumber company placed a lien on the land. (So now I learned what a lien was! Years in a monastery had not prepared me for certain things.)

I persuaded my various creditors to accept partial monthly payments. My past record of prompt payment was an advantage. Even so, however, the least that I was able to get them to accept totaled $2,500 a month, for five months. In addition to this sum I had all my other normal expenses: apartment, car, books and correspondence office, classes, food, etc. My years in a monastery had not prepared me for this, either!

Or had they? Knowledgeable effort alone could not possibly have taken me over this hurdle. The only thing that seems to work in times of real crisis is faith in God. I plunged in, doing the best I could, and placed the outcome wholly in His hands.

More students than ever enrolled in the classes. Friends helped generously, even nobly. Every month, several times with very little to spare, my commitments of $2,500 were paid, and all my other expenses were met. At one point the lumber company, which I had been paying regularly according to our agreement, tried anyway to force a foreclosure. Miraculously, my income that month was greater than usual; I paid off the entire debt, and was left, after paying my other bills, with $1.37 in my bank account!

By the end of the year, the retreat had been not only built, but very nearly paid off. People were beginning to "rally round the flag." It was time to begin thinking seriously once again about forming our cooperative community.

Chapter Five

THE PURCHASE OF ANANDA FARM

As early as the end of 1967 a friend had volunteered to stay at Ananda and act as caretaker. By late summer, 1968, we were holding our first retreats in the barely completed buildings. Through the winter of that year several persons were already living at the retreat as hermits.

It was in February, 1969, that we held our second meeting in San Francisco to discuss forming a community. By this time, interest and confidence in the venture had grown strong. The question was no longer whether, but *how*, to begin. The decisions reached in that second meeting, and in others that followed shortly after it, have to a large extent had to be altered as experience has taught us greater wisdom. But a start was at least made then, and by the spring of 1969 the first families began arriving at Ananda.

Our plan, as I have already said, was only to *start* the family aspect of the community at the Retreat, and after a couple of years or so, when we had grown stronger, to buy land for it elsewhere – perhaps, I thought, in the area of Auburn, fifty miles to the south, where the planting season is longer.

God had other plans for us, however, and to set

our minds thinking in the right direction He sent us some particularly noisy children at the very outset. Meditations in the temple became a backdrop of silent disapproval to gleeful shouts, angry accusations, and bitter tears over which no one had the slightest control. Auburn was too far away for such a fledgling community. I began wondering whether suitable land might not be found nearby – and soon.

Dick Baker at this time became worried that we might not, despite the best of intentions, be strong enough within two years or so to move the families away from the Retreat. After all, my assurances were based on *my* faith, not on his. And so it happened that just now, when we were on the point of starting our cooperative community in earnest, and were at last completely out of debt, I received a letter from Dick asking me to undertake no further construction until we could meet and discuss things in person. Unfortunately, he was in Japan, and was not expected to return until autumn. It was still only June. His request seemed catastrophic.

In fact, however, it proved a real blessing.

I received his letter on a Friday morning. That afternoon I drove up to Ananda from my San Francisco apartment, and stopped off in Sacramento on the way to visit a friend of mine, Dr. Gordon Runnels, in his office. While I was there another friend of his, a real estate agent, stopped by, and began speaking excitedly about what he called "the hottest land buy I've ever seen." I asked him where it was. He replied, "In the hills north of Auburn."

And where north of Auburn? He drew out a map to show me. It was of our area! The acreage he was pointing to, in fact, was located only a few minutes' drive from Ananda Retreat.

"The owner," he told me, "is a terminal cancer patient. He wants to settle his affairs as quickly as possible. His land has been subdivided, mostly into forty-acre parcels. It isn't even on the market yet, but already the guys in the office are beginning to place options on pieces of it for themselves, and are getting their friends interested."

"I'm going up very near there this afternoon," I told him. "Would you like to come along and show me this land?"

So it was that, in the fading daylight, we found ourselves walking over some of the most beautiful countryside I have ever seen in my life – a life that has taken me twice around the world, and to some forty different countries.

"Would you be able," I asked him, "to hold a few pieces for me over the weekend?" I mentioned which pieces, specifically, I wanted; they amounted to most of the property.

"I'll try," he replied.

The down payment for the parcels that I wanted came to $13,500 – an unthinkably high sum for which to raise even promises over one weekend. "But," I said, "if God wants us to have it, He should have no problem working things out for us."

It has never been my good fortune to attract wealthy sponsors, perhaps because of a deep-seated fear of being owned. But I know many people, and a few of them have at least *some* money. I got busy on the telephone. By Saturday morning, less than twenty-four hours after receiving Dick Baker's discouraging letter, I had promises of loans and gifts totalling exactly $13,500.

"To play it safe," the real estate agent told me Saturday morning when I phoned him, "I went into the office at two o'clock last night. It's lucky that I did so. I was able to reserve all the parcels you wanted, but this morning five or six of the other fellows came and pleaded with me to let them have some of your parcels. By getting those promises of help so quickly, you've acted just in time, I can tell you. What you've done is snatch that land right out from everyone else's noses."

There was still the matter of talking over this purchase with our present members. They all agreed, however, that it was the only possible step to take at this time. And so it was that we acquired well over 200 acres of additional land for our families, farming, and heavier industries. This new land became known as Ananda Farm. It is only six miles from Ananda Meditation Retreat – close enough to have remained a part of the same community.

Interestingly, almost all of the original promises of money for the down payment fell through. We needed the initial confidence which those promises gave us, but God had other ways of raising the down payment when it actually came due.

The story of the farm purchase had a particularly poignant ending. It had saddened me to think that our good fortune was coming to us at the cost of the former owner's life. Sometime later I met his doctor, who happens to have married the daughter of some friends of my family when we lived in Scarsdale, New York. He told me that this man's cancer, which had indeed been terminal, had been quite marvellously cured not long after we had taken possession of the land.

Chapter Six

COMMUNAL BEGINNINGS

Ananda Cooperative Community really started, at least in its present form, with the purchase of Ananda Farm. It began with an explosion which we very nearly didn't survive.

The news spread by an amazingly efficient underground grapevine that a new "commune" had been started and needed members. People began arriving from everywhere. One afternoon alone there were seven cars in our driveway, full of people wanting to join Ananda. Many of this horde were the usual drop-outs, seekers, not for a positive way of life, but for a soft berth. They ate our food, ran up our phone bill, and told us how we ought to be living. Most of them required our time and attention. A few of them, of course, we actually wanted with us as members.

For of course we did need members. What we didn't need was an invasion. We had to get the word out as quickly as possible by the ever-efficient grapevine that Ananda was not at all "where it's at." It took awhile, but we were relieved at last to find ourselves being dubbed in certain circles as "up tight," materialistic, not a real "commune." And in other circles, we were grateful to learn, people were beginning to think of us as dedicated, responsible, sincere. In short, Ananda began to develop its own "image", increasingly, those who came even as visitors were to be those who were in tune with us.

Perhaps my own greatest struggle in the beginning stemmed from the fact that we had to admit enough members to make the Farm economically possible. Many of these newcomers were people who had no knowledge of the background of Ananda, nor any special desire to help me, as its founder, to fulfill my dreams for it. Their attitude was perfectly understandable. A basic principle on which the community had been founded, in fact, was that no member would have more than one vote. That, of course, included me. It was important for me to adhere to this principle if I didn't want Ananda to turn into a dictatorship.

Yet it was also true that I had spent years growing into ideas that most of these newcomers had never even considered before. Many of my so-called dreams for Ananda were, I at least knew, essential to its very survival. Others were necessary to my own continued interest in the community. In addition to wanting to impress upon our members certain ideas that I knew to be vital to its success and future growth, I wanted to educate them to the thought of accepting real responsibility for managing their own affairs. For I had determined from the start to stick to my original notion of not becoming the community's manager.

Partly by working personally with those members who showed a willingness to assume definite responsibility, partly by offering sound enough reasons for my proposals, and partly by laying constant stress on our spiritual directions, I was able in time to accomplish my objectives. More and more, the community took on the character I had dreamed of in founding it, even to managing its own affairs in an admirable and responsible manner.

One of our first struggles was over the question of drugs, which every newcomer to the community had promised not to take, but which soon began to exercise an attraction again for certain people, especially when things became outwardly difficult. There were a couple of times when I had to be firm, even to asking one person to leave, but on the whole I felt that reason, and a growing spiritual force in the community, would solve the problem for us. Eventually my expectations proved justified.

Another problem was one of the community's self-identity. Many of the members wanted, or at least expected, Ananda to develop as a close-knit family unit, a sort of "tribe." Gradually, however, our people came to experience for themselves the truth, which I have stressed in this book, that a fair measure of privacy is spiritually desirable, as well as conducive to communal harmony. Thus, without very much difficulty, the community decided on its own that it wanted to become more what this book suggests, an intentional village, rather than a typical "commune."

When we first moved to Ananda, so our neighbors later told us, word quickly spread through the surrounding community that "bad news" had come to Nevada County. But we came wishing to become responsible citizens and good neighbors. Soon the general impression changed. People found that we respected local laws and authorities, paid our bills promptly, and added a certain positive aura of our own to the area. A surprisingly large number of people, moreover, though not members of our community, have moved to Nevada

County as a direct consequence of our being here. All in all, Ananda has been good for local business. The good will that we have received from the surrounding community stands in sharp contrast to the local hostility that a number of other communities have encountered.

Much more remarkable than harmony with people outside the community is the harmony of the members within it. Very rarely now is there any friction among them. Part of the reason for this, certainly, is that our members are men and women of good will. Yet even people of good will have been known not to get along well together. I think it must be added, therefore, that our members are developing, through their daily meditations, a spiritual maturity which puts their relations with one another on a higher plane.

This growing spiritual maturity reflects itself in their management of community affairs. It is the greatest single reason why, despite Ananda's chaotic beginnings, its direction of growth has been steadily toward greater harmony, cooperation, and a sense of true spiritual kinship.

Chapter Seven

FINANCIAL PROBLEMS

The history of Ananda from its inception has, alas, been intimately connected with a struggle over finances. Our purchase of the farm meant an assumption of payments in the amount of $1,750 a month – in direct contradiction to my own advice in this book that new communities try to stay out of debt. But we really had no other choice. And my experiences so far had given me some reason for believing that God would continue to open the way for us, whenever He limited our choices as strictly as He had this time.

Again and again in my life God has shown me that the greatest calamities, if accepted with faith in Him, are the very doorway through which He chooses to send His greatest blessings. Either He has a very twisted sense of humor, or this is His way of developing our faith! For faith is a dynamic thing. It must be *exercised*; it cannot be merely entertained, like some pleasing sentiment. (It should be added, however, that one's exercise of it must be commensurate with one's actual experience of its powers. Otherwise it will become mere presumption, and will usually be ineffectual.)

The mortgage payments, a heavy burden at first,

proved in time to be one of the principal and most necessary factors in drawing the community together. For money was, at the beginning, a bad word to most of our members. It spelled materialism, ego, worldliness – everything that we were trying to outgrow. Many of our people had yet to learn that lethargy, too, is a form of materialism – far worse so, in fact, than money madness; that a non-productive life is destructive to spiritual consciousness; and that money is only a form of energy: It can be used wisely, as well as misused. As I consider the (for me) immense amounts of money that I had to make or raise in getting Ananda started, I am continually astonished at the fact that my real gain from those painful struggles has been inward, not outward. To work hard to materialize a high ideal is not materialism. God had given us Ananda Farm with a strict condition attached to it. If we wanted to hang onto our blessing, we had to work hard to pay for it. A growing love for the community and for our environment induced the members to begin to work earnestly at various self-supportive industries. Gradually, they came to discover that their work was a valid form of service, and as such a source of great inner blessings for themselves.

It took awhile to develop this understanding. I moved to Ananda in June, 1969. My fond expectation was that many people working together would free me of the need to be out in the cities all the time teaching yoga classes. But at first people simply did not work together. In fact, some of them didn't even work. And those who did work, and hard, could not generate any real income at the very outset; it takes time to establish a profitable business.

Things were coming together, if slowly. They only

hadn't "clicked" yet. But there was a time, towards the end of 1969, when everything came close to disintegrating completely. Winter was coming, and most of our people didn't know how they would face it. The mortgage payments had been deferred because the sellers had not yet put in certain roads which they had promised us. Suddenly we received notices of intent to foreclose. Few of our members could even think in terms of such large sums of money. Drugs became an escape for some of them. People retreated into a kind of fantasy world with regard to the mortgage: If God wanted it paid, *He* would take care of it. This was certainly the bleakest period in our history.

I decided to give some people time to come to grips with reality, and others time to get their industries going. I had no intention of spending my life working away from Ananda just so that others might live there and play. It was particularly trying to me to find that a few people saw in my willingness to work for them the very justification for their own faith that God would, somehow, take care of them. I agreed to assume the responsibility for paying the mortgage only through May, 1970. Thus, I lived in Sacramento through the winter months, teaching classes again.

The hardest blow for me came when, after paying regularly on the mortgage for four months, I received a notice that if within two weeks I didn't pay, in addition, all those back payments, the property would be foreclosed. I had thought we would win a waiver on the grounds that the sellers had not fulfilled their promises. I was powerless, however, to force my point. In two weeks, in other words, I had to come up with an *additional* $4,500 or we'd lose the whole Farm.

"Face it," a friend of mine said the evening that

I received this letter, "you can't win 'em all."

"Come on over to my place," another friend urged me, "and have some tea. It will make you feel better."

"What do you mean?" I cried. "I'm not interested in how I *feel* about this! I'm interested in what I can *do* about it!"

I probably looked stunned; I certainly felt it. But the right time to console oneself with feelings of non-attachment is certainly not during the thick of a battle. So long as even half a day still remained, I had at least a chance to succeed. In fact, I was inwardly certain of success.

When I returned home that night, I began making a round of urgent telephone calls. I managed to defer the foreclosure a month and a half longer. The final payment to forestall it was due June 1st. With God's grace, I paid it, along with the regular mortgage payment for that month, on May 31st.

I then moved back to Ananda, and turned the responsibility for further mortgage payments over to the entire community.

The members in the meantime had grown spiritually, as well as in practical sense. I returned to find the morale high, the industries promising, and the love for our way of life now strong enough for people to want to make the sacrifices necessary to preserve it.

For myself, I must admit that I had reached a point of exhaustion. For the remainder of that summer it was all I could do to give retreat classes. After years of fund-raising activities, the time had come, I felt, for me to go more deeply into myself.

A spur in this direction came a month after my return to Ananda. In the early morning hours of July 3rd, our Retreat temple burned down. It was uninsured;

the loss to us was considerable.

But again there were fortunate consequences. We all need a few hardships in life to encourage us to strengthen our grip on positive attitudes. In that sense, this was a golden opportunity. Later that day a couple of us entered a nearby grocery store.

"You are singing!" exclaimed the proprietress, a French woman. "When our house burn down last year, I cry and cry for six months!"

But after all, why *not* sing? To identify one's happiness with mere things is to live in bondage. The loss of the temple, in fact, brought me inner blessings that went far beyond any personal determination to keep "a stiff upper lip." I felt a deep inner reassurance, and a stronger conviction than ever that nothing in life matters except serving and pleasing God. From now on, too, I knew that God wanted me to work more intensively on building my own, inner "temple."

The labor of rebuilding the temple, and the affirmation of courage that it entailed, helped substantially to bring our people together. This loss in fact, like many other hardships, in time proved a real blessing. We had new members by now who were familiar with the problems of constructing geodesic domes. The new temple is larger and much more beautiful than the first.

As for me, increasingly since the temple burned down I have entered a life of seclusion. For months now, in fact, I have been coming out only on weekends to speak. As it has turned out, my seclusion has proved more helpful to Ananda than my strenuous efforts at fund raising ever did, and has also given people an incentive to work harder so as to make it possible for me to remain here full time.

These last nine years have been a struggle. But as I tell people, even if, after all these efforts, Ananda were to fail, I would feel that I had gained permanent benefits from all this work. Outward things come and go. Worldly success and failure are inextricably bound to each other. The gains that are lasting are within. Ultimately, they are the sole reason for all our outward labors.

Sunday worship service in the new temple.

Chapter Eight

LESSONS LEARNED

Many are the lessons that these past years have taught me. In a sense, what I have learned seems too personal to have included among the suggestions in the first part of this book. But they may be useful to some readers who want to follow the same route of starting a community. Let us therefore consider a few of these lessons here.

When the religious organization to which I had belonged threw me out with stern warnings never to return, I felt for a long time that I had lost my reason for living. There was simply no imaginable disaster for me that could be greater than this one. But I have learned that divine grace grows only in the soil of hearts that have been softened by suffering.

People often tend to give up after a few hardships. If they have some faith in God, they will often say, "These obstacles prove that He doesn't want me to go in this direction." Well, they may or they may not prove it. If you see ample signs of His support in other ways, or if you feel inwardly sure of His support, obstacles and hardships may actually be marks of His favor, of His desire to help you to grow strong. The important thing is *not to be afraid* to sacrifice for the things in life that are worthwhile to you. Triumph always implies a struggle. Life's easy satisfactions bring us no inner growth, and soon prove stultifying to the soul.

The thrice-repeated loss of my first geodesic dome, which was to be my own home, taught me a lesson that I think may prove helpful to others who want to start communities: Build for others first, and only then for yourself.

The opposition that I encountered when I first proposed the actual formation of a cooperative community forced me to follow a line of approach that I think might also prove helpful to others. Whatever the central aim of your community is to be, I suggest that you build first with a view to focusing the community's consciousness there. In our case, since our ideal was spiritual growth, the fact of having a temple first was vital to our future development.

Essential to our own development also was the publication of this book, for it gave everyone a chance to see and to understand where we were headed. If you propose to use this book as a basis for a community of your own, it would help you to insist that all your prospective members study it, if only to help them to arrive at a clearer concensus concerning the directions they themselves want to go.

I have always felt that one reason God made it possible for me to meet all my financial obligations, some of which were so staggering (during most of my adult life, my allowance, as a monk, had been only $20 a month!), was that I never allowed even the severest pressures to tempt me to think of getting from people, rather than giving to them. If they couldn't afford to take my classes, I let them attend anyway in exchange for some simple service, such as setting up the room for a class, or spending a weekend working at Ananda. Some people took advantage of my leniency, but I knew that it was God, not man, from whom my help was really coming. I believe that others would find it helpful, similarly, to place service first at *all* times, and not to think that a good cause justifies a temporary consciousness of greed.

One mistake I made in trying to interest people in Ananda was to present them at the outset with too sweeping a plan. Most people require time to grow into a new idea. Indeed, probably most people are never as stirred by the thought of a challenge as the kind of person who goes about starting things. If you want to start a community, therefore, you would probably do well not to let the presentation of your vision get too far ahead of the actual situation at hand. One step at a time is the safest policy.

Our direction of development at Ananda has several times forced us to take steps that are in opposition to some of the recommendations in this book. We assumed a heavy debt, for example, when we acquired Ananda Farm, though I've recommended that no new community do so. We abandoned from the outset an idea that I proposed in earlier editions of this book, namely, that the community be the sole employer; and another, taken from B.F. Skinner's *Walden Two*, that workers be paid at least partly in the form of negotiable chits, rather than in cash. Both ideas proved more cumbersome than useful. It wasn't long, in fact, before we decided to adopt the system we had all grown up with and understood: to have separate, privately owned industries, and to let other people work in them for pay.

In the early editions of this book I suggested selling shares in the community as a means of developing it. This has proved unfeasible for us, and indeed I no longer recommend it for others.

We have made changes also in our set-up of the governing body. What appears now in this book in the chapter on government is substantially the system we now follow, but in earlier editions I suggested something more elaborate – much *too* elaborate for a group of people whose main wish in living together is to live simply.

People often ask us how we have been so successful, particularly when so many similar communities have fallen apart. Many reasons might be advanced, but I think of these the most important are three: 1) We find our peace inwardly first, in meditation, and only secondarily from one another; 2) we have learned that the secret of work is joyous service; and 3) we have learned that to see God in one another, and in all men, is to dissolve all sense of differences between us and them. People are often astonished at how little friction there is here. But there is really no mystery about that. Inner peace, like an oil, keeps the machinery of life flowing smoothly, all its parts working together harmoniously.

People sometimes ask us, What about our plans for the future? How large do we want to grow? What responsibility do we feel toward the cooperative community movement as a whole? Do we hope to open branches of Ananda Cooperative Community elsewhere?

Our plans for the future include a spiritually oriented, "How-to-Live" school, patterned after the ideas in this book, and as much as possible after the educational ideals of our Guru, Paramahansa Yogananda. The school will begin as a high school, open to children from outside the community. It will be situated on fifteen acres of land that we have acquired for this purpose, adjacent to, and yet (because of the topography) separate from the Farm property. I refer to this as a future project because we have as yet constructed no buildings for the school, but in fact, in spite of this minor handicap, we do already have a small high school, complete with accredited teachers, operating for the time being at Ananda Retreat. Students from outside the community live in retreat cabins, which are less in demand by retreatants during the cooler months of the year. We plan to place the school under The Yoga Fellowship, a non-profit religious corporation that I founded in 1968. In this way we hope to attract tax-deductible donations for the construction of the school buildings, and for further development. At the time of this writing, the legalities are in the process of being worked out. I hope that the generous reader, if he likes our educational ideas well enough to want to help further them, will bear us in mind for possible contributions.

Another plan for the near future is evolving from the fact that a growing number of our members are coming to feel attracted to the monastic ideal. It has long, in fact, been my belief that a monastic group functioning within the broader framework of a cooperative community would help immeasurably to strengthen the over-all sense of spiritual purpose. Sadhus, or holy men, that live permanently in proximity to an Indian village are accounted a blessing on the whole community. Their renunciation inspires householders to cling less firmly to the thought of "me and mine."

My reason for starting a secular community first was not only because this is a special need of our

times (there are numerous monasteries already in existence), but also because I felt, if I was going to start a secular community at all, that it would be unwise to try to develop it out of a monastic order. Inharmony would almost certainly result, even as it would in the life of an individual if he abandoned a completely dedicated for a more self-centered way of life. The monks would see in the lives of the more recently arrived householders a betrayal of their selfless principles. The householders would resent the monks for what they considered their narrow-mindedness. The monks, in setting the tone for the whole community, would seek to impose an unreasonable strictness on everyone. And the householders, if they were not cowed into becoming mere sheep in their obedience (forgive the mixed metaphor; I couldn't resist it!), would probably set themselves in a determined attitude of rebellion. This, at least, is a pattern that I have had some opportunity to observe over the years.

The natural line of evolution is from the lower to the higher: in this case, from the secular to the spiritual. In India, where this fact is understood, there is rarely any friction between householders and monks, for it is felt that the latter are a blessing on the established order, rather than the householders being a misfortune to it.

Thus it was that I wanted to found Ananda first as a secular community. Now, however, that it has been founded and is flourishing, the time has arrived for us to add to our existing structure a monastic order. We have called this new order "The Friends of God." It has started with ten Ananda members: seven men and three women.

We have not set an absolute limit for the number of residents at Ananda, but I think a fair estimate would be about 200 persons, including children. Of this number, not more than forty persons would live at the Retreat. Even 200 residents would probably exceed our actual needs as a community, but it would permit the training of groups to send elsewhere for the formation of new communities.

Yes, we do plan to start other communities elsewhere. But as I have recommended in this book, each community will be autonomous; in this sense, it will not be a branch of Ananda, but an equal member of a kind of loose-knit fraternity.

As for our sense of responsibility to the cooperative community movement as a whole, it is in no way our desire to "make the scene." Our interests are practical. People who want to involve us in lengthy discussions on "theories" of communal living usually find that our answers are circumscribed by the expression, "Well, this is what we have found works." That, essentially, is the approach of this book: not the spinning of merely beautiful, but of *workable*, ideas.

Chapter Nine

"HERE AND NOW"

It is Tuesday, July 13, 1971, as I write these lines. The day has been pleasantly warm, not hot; the sky has remained all day without a cloud. I lay in a Mexican hammock for awhile before returning to write this last chapter, and gazed peacefully across a wide valley at the high Sierra in the distance. Fading patches of snow still cling, as if pleading for protection, to the higher slopes. I imagined myself for a moment back in the Himalayas. And then I smiled. Why be anywhere in the world but right here, right now? Philosophically speaking, of course, that is always a good thought; but it is one that comes particularly naturally here at Ananda.

For months now I have enjoyed the seclusion I sought so longingly nine years ago. Will you say that it has taken me long enough to find it? But what are nine years? I consider that part of my life well spent. These have been years of inner growth as well as, perhaps, of some outward usefulness.

Life drifts by so quickly, almost unnoticeably, like a cloud. I know that this seclusion I now enjoy will not last indefinitely. Life itself will not last. I pray that, when my time comes to leave this world, it will be with a mental sky quite as empty of any clouds of attachment or desire as the sky above me has been this day. For what kind of home can we build here on earth? Ananda will flourish for a time. When it has fulfilled its purpose, it will go. To desire perfection in the outer world is a delusion. Only as a place for making great *inner* strides can Ananda fulfill its true purpose.

The time is 5:45. Residents and retreatants have just finished practicing energization exercises and yoga postures together on the deck outside the temple, about 150 feet from my house. A few moments ago I heard their footsteps as they entered the temple for meditation before supper. Later this evening they will gather again, to chant, meditate, offer healing prayers for others, and listen to a reading from one of the writings of our great Guru, Paramahansa Yogananda.

Every now and then the sound of a distant truck, or of an airplane overhead, breaks in upon the silence to remind us that that other world still exists "out there." More often what one hears is a bird singing, a lizzard scurrying up a tree trunk, a bee pausing briefly at a blossom in flight.

A typical day at Ananda Meditation Retreat begins at six o'clock with exercise and meditation. No one is obliged to attend. Group activities are offered as a benefit, not as a rule, of membership. A few of our people prefer to meditate on their own. Breakfast, except on weekends, is at 8:00. There is another meditation at noon.

Soon after breakfast, work begins. Some of our residents work here on the Retreat grounds. Others go to the Farm to work, whether at farming, or in one of our various industries. Ananda members make incense, health candy bars, artistic jewelry, pottery, clothing. They print books (including this one). They paint. They weave. They build geodesic domes. Anyone with a skill of his own is encouraged to put it to use. Ananda products are becoming increasingly popular in stores throughout California. Perhaps you have seen them?

Financially, at last, we are holding our own.

Life at the Farm is more hectic than at the Retreat. But hectic is a relative word. You go into the incense factory. The workers, some of them softly singing a devotional chant, look up and smile. As likely as not no words are exchanged; smiles are more eloquent.

Some of our members have asked me to give them Indian names. Jyotish, who founded the incense business a year and a half ago, functions informally also as the community's general manager. Capable, perceptive, marvellously patient – I think a large measure of our success is due to him.

And then I think how fortunate we are in this other person, and in that, and before I know it the list has grown too long for me to maintain a sharp focus on anyone. What makes us truly fortunate, I reflect, is that in this lifetime so many have been drawn to seek and to serve God.

Sonia, who held an important job in the city, and helped me substantially during my financial crisis in 1968, works now as our treasurer and general office manager. Her happy smile is a blessing on the community.

Haanel, our head farmer, is probably also our most erudite member. An elderly man with a delightful insight into the vagaries of life, he has been a famous photographer, and a hermit in Chilean jungles, as well as farming his own land in Vista, California. He came here two years ago. It is because of his expertise that we now have a flourishing farm.

Satya came here three years ago; he has been in charge of the Retreat ever since. Thanks to his steadfastness, the scheduled activities here flow smoothly the year around.

Most of our adults are in their twenties or early thirties. About seventy people, including children, presently live at the two places. But the number is growing. Even now at the Retreat there are several guests who hope to become permanent members.

Requirements for membership are that one be a disciple, or at least a sincere devotee, of our Guru, Paramahansa Yogananda, and of his line of gurus; that one have studied, or be in the process of studying, our Guru's correspondence course lessons from Self-Realization Fellowship in Los Angeles, and also our own yoga correspondence course from Ananda; that one be definitely and completely off of hallucinogenic drugs and alcoholic beverages; that one be able to pay his membership fee ($1,000 for single persons, $1,500 for married couples) upon acceptance, and be able in addition to pay for the construction of his own residence; that there be gainful employment for him in the community; and above all, that the community members feel an attunement with him and accept him.

After two years, we are finally on the verge of incorporating Ananda as a cooperative society. Our experience heretofore was inadequate to permit us to take this step. In some ways we regret having to take it now, but we know that it is necessary. Other formalities will probably become necessary also, as we grow. One reason we don't want to grow too large is so that we may keep our way of life as simple and as free of formalities as possible.

But life is a procession of seasons. New residents here often fear the approach of winter, but in the midst of it many of them find it even more beautiful than the summer months. So can life's changes be, if we accept them with inner peace.

This morning I had to break my silence to make a necessary phone call at the Farm. Upon returning, I noticed Satya sitting in the office, smiling, and looking particularly at peace with himself.

''You look happy,'' I said.

''How could one feel otherwise,'' he asked, ''living here?''